D1515507

GREAT COMPOSERS

BACH

JAMES PRENDERGAST LIBRARY
509 CHERRY STREET
JAMESTOWN, NEW YORK 14701

GREAT COMPOSERS

BACH

TIM DOWLEY

CHARTWELL
BOOKS, INC.

For copyright reasons this edition is for sale only within
the U.S.A.

This edition published in 1990 by
Chartwell Books, Inc.
a division of Book Sales, Inc.
110 Enterprise Avenue
Secaucus, New Jersey 07094

Prepared by The Hamlyn Publishing Group Limited
a division of The Octopus Publishing Group
Michelin House, 81 Fulham Road, London SW3 6RB

© 1990 The Hamlyn Publishing Group Limited

ISBN 1 55521 6064

Produced by Mandarin Offset

Printed in Hong Kong

CONTENTS

BACH
AND
THE BACHS

Johann Sebastian Bach came from a great clan of craftsman-musicians; yet with his astonishing musicianship he towers above them all.

That Johann Sebastian Bach became a musician was no surprise; that he became a composer of genius was. Bach came of a family of musicians; it has been estimated that, between the 16th and mid-19th centuries, a total of 75 Bachs made at least part of their living from music. But most of them were minor musicians – violinists in town bands, church organists, choirmasters or church cantors. Possibly half-a-dozen Bachs attained more than merely local fame – the family had deep roots in the region of Thuringia – but only Sebastian stands out as an original.

He was born at Eisenach, Thuringia, on 21 March 1685. Two days later his birth was recorded in the town's church book: 'To Mr Johann Ambrosius Bach, Town Musician, a son . . . Joh. Sebastian'. Thuringia, a hilly, wooded region, lies north of Bavaria and south of the Harz mountains, and is today part of the German Democratic Republic. In the 17th century its main towns included Gotha, Weimar, Erfurt, Jena and Eisenach, and it was traversed by the main routes

Left *Johann Ambrosius Bach (1645–95), father of Sebastian.*

Opposite *Johann Sebastian Bach at 30: an unauthenticated portrait by J.E. Rentsch.*

between Frankfurt to the west and Leipzig, Warsaw, Prague and Budapest to the east; and between Hamburg to the north and Nuremburg, Munich and Italy to the south.

EISENACH

Eisenach, Bach's birthplace, is today also remembered as the location of Martin Luther's secret refuge, when he was outlawed by the Diet of Worms in 1521. The great Protestant reformer hid in the fortress of the Wartburg, which overlooks Eisenach, occupying himself in translating the Bible into German and writing hymns.

Johann Ambrosius Bach (1645–95) was court trumpeter for the Duke of Eisenach and director of the town musicians. Germany was at this time still a patchwork of

little states, dukedoms, principalities and free cities; each ruler needed his own musicians; each town or city its band or orchestra, responsible for providing music at the town's main church and at civic events; the churches themselves also appointed organists, cantors, and directors of music.

Johann Ambrosius, whose chief instrument was the violin, is not known to have been a composer. In 1668 he married Maria Elisabeth Lämmerhirt, daughter of a town councillor at Erfurt, where he was then a town musician. Sebastian was their eighth and youngest child; four of his siblings died young.

The young boy may have learned the rudiments of fiddling from his father, the professional violinist, while it is possible that his first contact with the organ came through his second cousin, Johann Christoph Bach, who was the organist at St

Bach's birthplace: the town of Eisenach, Thuringia, in the south-west corner of what is now East Germany; from a 17th-century line engraving.

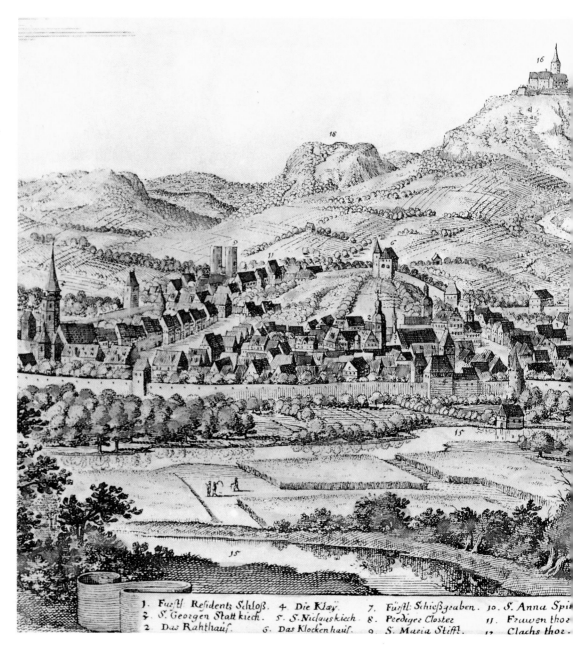

1. Fürstl. Residentz Schloß. 4. Die Klaß. 7. Fürstl. Schießgraben. 10. S. Anna Spi
2. S. Georgen Statt kirch. 5. S. Niclauskirch. 8. Prediger Closter. 11. Frauen thor
3. Das Rahthauß. 6. Das Klockenhauß. 9. S. Maria Stifft. 12. Clachs thor

Left *The Wartburg fortress overlooking Eisenach, where Martin Luther (below) hid at a dangerous period during the Reformation.*

. Georgenthor.   16. Schloß und Vestung Wartenberg.
Predigerthor.   17. Der Modelstein, da zuvor ein Schloß gestande
ie Nuß und Hersel fluß. 18. H c ist die Eisenacher burg gestanden

Right *Interior of the Bachs' home in Eisenach.*

Below *The front door of the Bach family's house.*

A bedroom in the Bach's home, Eisenach.

George's church, Eisenach, in 1642–95, and organist and harpsichordist to the Duke of Eisenach. Sebastian was clearly aware from his earliest years that he had been born into a clan of musicians, and later in life drew up a genealogy of his family, and he managed to trace back previous generations of musician Bachs.

At about the age of eight Sebastian entered the Eisenach grammar school (Martin Luther's old school), where several other Bachs had preceded him. Tuition lasted from seven till nine in the morning, and from one till three in the afternoon, with an additional hour's lessons on winter mornings. The young Bach was taught Latin, German grammar, arithmetic, logic, the Catechism and the Scriptures. He also sang in the church choir at St George's, having

what was described as 'an uncommonly fine treble voice'.

OHRDRUF

In May 1694 Sebastian's mother died; in January 1695, less than a year later, and only three months after remarrying, his father died, leaving his new wife, Barbara Margaretha, a widow for the third time. Sebastian was still only 10 years old. However, in a society hardened to frequent mortalities, the extended family often came to the aid of orphans. In this case, Sebastian and his 13-year-old brother, Johann Jakob, were sent to Ohrdruf, 30 miles south-east of Eisenach, to live with their eldest brother, Christoph, who had left

11

Line engraving of Ohrdruf, where Bach lived with his brother Johann Christian.

home when Sebastian was barely one year old. Johann Christoph Bach (1671–1721), now 23, newly-married and the organist at St Michael's church, Ohrdruf, had studied the organ and harpsichord at Erfurt under the accomplished organist and composer Johann Pachelbel (1653–1706), whose canon has brought him latter-day fame.

It was at Ohrdruf, and probably under his brother Christoph's eye, that Sebastian began to play the organ. When a new organ was installed at the Ohrdruf church, Christoph allowed his young brother to watch its construction. He also encouraged him to study composition; although no composer himself, he set Sebastian to copying music by German organist/composers such as Jakob Froberger, Johann Caspar Kerll and Pachelbel. (A possibly apocryphal story – one of a genre that seems to spring up around infant composers – tells that Christoph punished his young brother when he discovered he had copied a forbidden musical manuscript by moonlight. We do not know enough about this incident to justify the allegations of harshness that have been laid against Christoph).

The boy was able to contribute to his upkeep by earning fees singing in the Chorus Musicus of Ohrdruf, a choir of about 20 voices. He resumed his education at the Ohrdruf grammar school, and did much better in class. Daily theology, Latin and German were combined with music four times a week under the cantor, Johann Heinrich Arnold, described in the school records as 'a menace to the school, a scandal to the church, and a cancer in the community'. The position of cantor – one which Sebastian was himself later to hold at Leipzig – combined the duties of teaching in school and organising the musical activities of the town.

LÜNEBERG

Fortunately Arnold was eventually sacked and replaced by the less formidable Elias Herda, a young man of 24, who had recently completed theological studies at the university of Jena. Herda managed to secure a free scholarship for Sebastian and his fellow-pupil Georg Erdmann at his *alma mater*, the charity school of St Michael's church, Lüneberg, 200 miles away in north Germany. This move was probably prompted by the increase in Christoph's family, which meant there was no longer enough room for Sebastian in his brother's house, or sufficient money to support him.

At Lüneberg, by singing treble in the matins choir – a select group of 12 to 15 voices within the larger church choir – Sebastian was able to earn a modest allowance of 12 groschen per month, in addition to the free board and tuition he

Opposite The interior of St Michael's church, Lüneberg, where as a boy Sebastian sang in the choir.

received under the terms of his scholarship. Additional dates to sing at weddings, funerals and other occasions were welcome since they supplemented his income.

St Michael's church had fine musical traditions; a considerable library of music had been built up, started by the first Protestant cantor, and steadily enlarged over the years. Sebastian doubtless drew upon these resources, and from the encouragement of finding a fellow Thuringian, Georg Böhm (1661–1733), organist at St John's church, Lüneberg. It has been argued that Bach's earliest organ compositions owe something to Böhm's influence. (One of Böhm's minuets was later copied into the *Little Keyboard Book* for Anna Magdalena Bach.)

Böhm was himself indebted musically to his own teacher, the renowned north German organist Johann Adam Reincken

(1623–1722), who still played regularly at St Catherine's church, Hamburg, although in his late 70s. On at least one occasion Bach walked the 30 miles from Lüneberg to Hamburg to meet Reincken and listen to his playing; the young student was probably more interested in the master's organ technique than his compositions, for Bach was already building the foundations of his own prodigious organ technique. The organ at St Catherine's had 51 stops, splendid reeds, and a fine 32 foot principal; more than Bach was to have at his disposal at any point in his career.

While at Lüneberg, Sebastian also grasped the opportunity of hearing contemporary French music. At his court at Celle the Duke of Brunswick-Lüneberg employed a French court musician, Thomas de la Selle, who attempted to imitate the fashionable sounds of the orchestra of the French

Johann Adam Reincken (1623–1722), the famous organist from Hamburg.

Right *The 18th-century German organ at Michaelsberg.*

Below *A sketch by Fragonard of 18th-century aristocrats making chamber music.*

The castle at Celle, where the Duke of Brunswick-Lüneberg emulated French styles in music and fashion.

court with a band of 16 players, only two of whom were German. Bach visited Celle, some 50 miles south of Lüneberg, and there observed French fashions and heard music by French composers such as Lully, Colasse and Destouches. He was clearly impressed by what he found, for the memoirs written by his son, Carl Philipp Emanuel, and by his pupil, Lorenz Mizler, recall Bach's anecdotes about the court at Celle. We know that Bach also made copies of French keyboard music by such composers as Nicolas de Grigny and Charles Dieupart. Theirs was a world utterly different from the grammar schools of Thuringia.

RETURN TO THURINGIA

Sebastian continued as a scholarship boy at St Michael's school for three years, possibly until his voice broke. After his enticingly novel experiences in the north, he returned to Thuringia, aged 18 and with no possibility of pursuing further education. When he heard of the vacant post of organist at St James's church, Sangerhausen, near Halle, he applied for it. Although it was accepted that he was the

best candidate, the church authorities were overruled by the local potentate, Johann Georg, Duke of Sachse-Weissenfels, who preferred an older applicant, Johann Augustine Kobelius, whose great-grandfather had been court organist at Weissenfels.

It seems that, as a result of this disappointment, the duke felt some obligation to the young Bach, and arranged for his employment as 'lackey and violinist' at the court of Duke Johann Ernst, younger brother of the ruling Duke of Weimar. For a short period Sebastian played the violin in the little court orchestra at Weimar, and assisted the ageing court organist, Johann Effler, who was a friend of the Bach family.

But young Sebastian had his eye on a vacant organist's post at Arnstadt, where the old church of St Boniface had burned down in 1581 and had been rebuilt a century later, when it became known as the New Church. However, 20 years after completion of the new church building, the new organ was still not ready for use, and no organist was yet needed. When the organ was finally finished, Bach received the chance he had been awaiting: the mayor of Arnstadt, a distant relative, persuaded the council to invite 'Mr Johann Sebastian Bach . . . to inspect the new organ in the New Church . . . July 13

1703.' Already young Bach seems to have gained a deserved reputation for testing and assessing the tuning and mechanics of organs. The instrument at Arnstadt, which boasted two manuals and 23 speaking stops, had been built by Johann Friedrich Wender of Mühlhausen; as part of his inspection of the new instrument, Sebastian gave a recital, which not only persuaded him of its quality, but also the council of his ability as an organist.

Bach was immediately appointed organist, with a contract stipulating he should:

appear promptly on Sundays, feast days, and other days of divine service in the New Church at the organ entrusted to you: to play it suitably: to keep a watchful eye over it and take good care of it; to report in good time if part of it becomes weak, and give warning to get the necessary repairs done; not to allow access to it

The organ of the New Church, Arnstadt, which Bach was asked to inspect in 1703.

Interior of the New Church, Arnstadt. Bach was appointed organist of the church after he had inspected the organ.

to anyone without the knowledge of the superintendent; generally to ensure that damage is avoided and everything kept in good order. Also in your daily life cultivate the fear of God, sobriety and love of peace; completely avoid bad company and anything which distracts you from

your calling, generally conducting yourself as towards God in all respects. . . .

Yet Bach's duties were far from burdensome. He had to play preludes and hymns on the organ every Sunday morning, as well as at the service of intercession on Monday,

and on Thursday morning. But he was organist and not choirmaster, as he had later to remind his employers; his contract did not require him to train or conduct the choir, a duty he never seems to have relished. At Arnstadt he had ample time to practise the organ and begin composing.

For his work as organist, Bach received a more than adequate salary of 50 florins a year, plus an allowance for board and lodging; as a youth of 18, he could be well satisfied. However, having secured a potentially promising position, the young musician faced a turbulent three years at Arnstadt. In part, this was due to his immaturity and his heady enthusiasm for new musical styles; in part, however, it was also due to the heavy-handedness of the Arnstadt authorities.

One of the many disputes with these authorities arose out of a trip Bach made to Lübeck in the autumn of 1705. He had obtained permission for a month's leave of absence, arranged for his cousin Johann Ernst to deputise for him, and then set out on the 250-mile journey north, which has been much mythologised in the re-telling. The attraction was the organ-playing of the great Dietrich Buxtehude (1637–1707) at St

Bach's organ console, the New Church, Arnstadt.

19

St Mary's church,
Lübeck, where
Bach heard the
great organist
Dietrich Buxtehude
play.

Mary's church. (Some writers have suggested that Bach harboured an ambition to succeed the 68-year-old master at St Mary's). But Bach was probably also attracted to Lübeck by the unique series of Vespers ('Abendmusik') directed by Buxtehude at St Mary's during the five Sundays of Advent, deploying some 40 instrumentalists. The musical style of the Vespers probably influenced Bach when he wrote his own church cantatas later, although the works peformed at Lübeck were extra-liturgical, and not even exclusively religious in character. Undoubtedly Bach was deeply impressed by this exposure to Buxtehude's virtuosity at the splendid organ at Lübeck: the rich registration that the master was able to achieve on the fine instrument at St Mary's, with its three manuals and 54 speaking stops, was never fully available to Bach on the more limited organs to which he had access during his own career.

When he eventually arrived back in Arnstadt in January 1706, having visited Reincken in Hamburg and Böhm in Lüneberg on his way, Bach had to face other, less welcome, music. He had been absent for over four months, rather than the one month negotiated, and now offered no apology or explanation to the Arnstadt authorities. (He had already been reprimanded the previous summer for his inability to get along with his students, his failure to rehearse them, and for his uncouth language during a street brawl with a student, the bassoonist Johann Heinrich Geyersbach, an incident which seems to typify Bach's unhappy relationship with the student choristers, whom the authorities claimed he was supposed to train.) Moreover, the congregation at Arnstadt were affronted by what seemed to them over-elaborate accompaniments to the hymns, unacceptable ornamentation, and generally too many flourishes and musical decorations emanating from Bach's organ loft.

In February 1706 Bach was called before the church consistory court and presented with an ultimatum:

Complaints have been made to the Consistory that you now accompany the hymns with surprising variations and irrelevant ornaments, which obliterate the melody and confuse the congregation. . . . We are surprised that you have given up performing music for voices and instruments, and assume that this is due to your bad relations with the pupils at the grammar school. We must therefore ask you to tell us explicitly that you are ready

to rehearse them in vocal and instrumental music, as well as in hymn-singing. We cannot provide a cantor, and you must tell us clearly whether you will do as we ask. If not, we must find an organist who will.

Bach could hardly misunderstand this blunt warning, despite the fact that his contract did not explicitly require him to conduct the choir. Nor is it surprising that his stay at Arnstadt was relatively short. It now seemed he could do no right: whereas the consistory had previously criticised him for overlong and complex preludes, now he was reprimanded for making them too short – maybe an instance of Bach's frequently stubborn reaction to criticism.

In November 1706 he was warned again:

The organist Bach . . . must declare, whether or not he is willing to make music with the students as already instructed; for, if he considers it no disgrace to be attached to the church and receive a salary, he must not be ashamed to make music with the students until directed otherwise.

To this warning was added another complaint: that Bach had invited a female stranger into the choir loft to sing. Bach had a ready answer; he informed his critic that he had informed the clergyman what he was doing. It is likely that the woman in question was Bach's cousin, Maria Barbara, who was soon to become his wife. Whoever it was, this seemed to be the last straw; the Arnstadt consistory were faced with an obstinate, self-willed young organist, who did not appear to be giving them value for money.

MÜHLHAUSEN

Although the rows apparently blew over, Bach was unsettled enough to start looking for a new position. The death in December 1706 of Johann Georg Ahle, organist at St Blasius' church, Mühlhausen, some 35 miles north-west of Arnstadt, offered Bach the opportunity he needed. He gave a trial performance at St Blasius', a church of cathedral-like proportions, on Easter Sunday 1707, and was subsequently offered the post. When asked to name his terms, he requested the same salary as he was receiving at Arnstadt (which was 20 gulden more than Ahle had been earning) together with the traditional payments in kind received by Ahle – 'three measures of corn, two trusses of wood, one of beech, one of oak or aspen, and six trusses of faggots, delivered to his door'. Bach took up his new duties at Mühlhausen on 14 September, having successfully negotiated his release from Arnstadt, where he was succeeded by his cousin, Johann Ernst.

Only a month after arriving in Mühlhausen, on 17 October 1707, Bach was married to Maria Barbara in the nearby village of Dornheim. Sebastian had been left a substantial legacy by his uncle, Tobias Lämmerhirt, in August; this probably put him in a sound enough position financially for him to propose marriage responsibly. Maria Barbara was the grand-daughter of Heinrich Bach (1615–92), sometime organist in Arnstadt and uncle of Johann Ambrosius, Sebastian's father.

The post at Mühlhausen was a step up from that in Arnstadt, and the new organist set to work immediately, copying out music with his pupil Johann Martin Schubart, playing for services, and composing music for special civic occasions, such as the annual inauguration of the town council in February 1708 – though his contract only required playing the organ at services.

This is the first real evidence we have of Bach as a composer, though there were one or two youthful pieces. We know of at least four works dating from his time at Mühlhausen: the well-known Easter piece, *Christ lag in Todesbanden*; a work for the council inauguration, *Gott ist mein König*; a funeral piece, *Gottes Zeit ist die allerbeste Zeit*; and there was a wedding cantata which he composed for the marriage of one of Maria Barbara's aunts, *Der Herr denket an uns*.

Gott ist mein König, written in the more ornamented style of Buxtehude, called for the full resources of the town musicians: Bach scored it for flutes, bassoons, oboes, drums and three trumpets, as well as string ensemble, chorus and organ, guaranteeing a brilliant effect. By contrast, *Christ lag in Todesbanden* is more solemn; it is based on a Lutheran chorale, with different verses set for various combinations of voices, and accompanied by strings.

As organist at St Blasius', Sebastian also took charge of improving the organ. With the experience gained at previous organ inspections and installations, he drew up a list of the instrument's shortcomings:

The parish church, Dornheim, where Bach and Maria Barbara were married in 1707.

The lack of wind must be overcome by adding three good new bellows. . . . The trombone bass must be fitted with new larger pipes, and the mouthpieces arranged quite differently to give the stop a solider tone. . . . The trumpet should be removed, and a fagotto . . . fitted, since it is invaluable for new ideas, and sounds fine in vocal and instrumental music.

In fact, much of his specification repeated the instructions Christoph Bach had made for the organ at St George's, Eisenach – with the additional novelty of a set of pedal-

The interior of St Blasius' church, Mühlhausen, where Bach was appointed organist in 1707.

operated chimes, requested by the parish.

What Bach does not seem to have bargained for at Mühlhausen was the strength of the Pietist religious movement. There was little liking at St Blasius' for advanced church music, and although the town authorities were well-pleased with the cantata *Gott ist mein König*, and had it printed (only one other of Bach's numerous cantatas was printed during his lifetime), the congregation and its pastor blocked and rejected the young organist's attempts to express his undoubted gifts.

The Pietist movement within Lutheranism stressed the importance of personal spiritual illumination, which it contrasted with the dead hand of doctrinal orthodoxy. The pastor at St Blasius', J.A. Frohne, was a well-known Pietist, and it is significant that

Bach's first child, born in December 1708, was baptised by Georg Christian Eilmar, pastor at St Mary's, Mühlhausen, and an outspoken opponent of Pietism. (Eilmar also provided the texts for a number of Bach's sacred cantatas).

In their desire for personal holiness, the Pietists cultivated an ascetic form of worship; they saw the excessive use of music or art in church as a snare to godliness, a temptation to worldliness. Some even called for a ban on instrumental music, which they saw as 'mixing the world's vanity with the sacred'. In following this trend, the church was moving in the opposite direction to Bach, who had already encountered opposition to his florid, decorative organ technique when at Arnstadt. Though Bach was an orthodox Lutheran, it is unlikely that

A 19th-century line engraving of St Blasius' church, Mühlhausen.

narrow, Puritanical or mystical beliefs held any attraction for him. For him music could enrich spirituality – not ensnare it.

Once again, Sebastian was seriously unsettled. The church where he held his appointment was quite out of sympathy with his technique and taste as a musician – if not with music in worship at all. Inevitably, he eventually resigned, in 1708, and gave an outline of the causes of his discontent:

I have not been allowed to do my work without opposition, and at present there is not the least appearance that things will improve. . . . In addition, if I may say it without disrespect, although my way of life is only modest, I do not earn enough to live on, after paying my rent and buying basic goods.

He also complained that the music he had successfully promoted in surrounding villages often surpassed that at St Blasius' – although there were people in the congregation who would have welcomed change!

Fortunately Bach did not have far to look for a new position. Johann Effler, organist at the Weimar court, was nearing retirement. When Duke Wilhelm Ernst of Saxe-Weimar offered Bach the post of organist and court musician, he immediately accepted. Here was an escape from the religious controversies of Arnstadt and Mühlhausen – and also the lure of a higher salary. Once more, there was no problem in negotiating release from his contract; Bach agreed to see through the refurbishment of the organ at Mühlhausen – and indeed returned to play his chorale *Ein' feste Burg* on the finished organ.

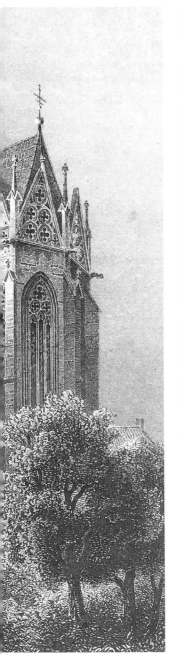

Bach's manuscript first page of his cantata Gott ist mein König, *composed at Mühlhausen.*

WEIMAR
AND
CÖTHEN

After troubled years of apprenticeship as a church organist, Bach now enjoyed the contrasting duties of a court musician at Weimar and Cöthen.

Bach's patron at Weimar, 40 miles east of Mühlhausen, was the rigidly orthodox Lutheran Duke Wilhelm Ernst, the older brother of Duke Johann Ernst, whom Bach had served briefly five years earlier. The duke affected cultural pursuits which he felt befitted his role – collecting fine books and coins, and encouraging music – but he was first and foremost a devout and serious-minded Christian, who insisted on the court joining him in his strict Lutheran observances. He did away with dances, tested his courtiers on the sermons preached in chapel, and insisted on early nights in the palace!

Bach's exact duties at Weimar are unclear; he certainly acted as organist and chamber musician, but did not attain the more exalted position of Kapellmeister. As a chamber musician, he had to wear a hussar's uniform, and probably played violin or viola. As organist he was free to practise, perform and compose, and he also persuaded the duke to have the chapel organ modified and reconstructed. In addition,

Bach was increasingly in demand as a tutor, to members of the ducal house, his own children, his Bach relations, and to other pupils, such as Johann Martin Schubart and Johann Tobias Krebs. At least at the outset, Sebastian escaped any responsibility for choirs or orchestral music.

It was during his nine years at Weimar that Bach found his feet as a composer and as a man; these were relatively contented years since he was openly appreciated by the duke, who increased his salary during his term of office.

The Bachs' first child, Catherina Dorothea, was born soon after they arrived in Weimar; two years later came Wilhelm Friedemann, born on 22 November 1710; short-lived twins in 1713; Carl Philipp Emanuel on 8 March 1714; and Johann Gottfried Bernhard on 11 May 1715. Wilhelm Friedemann (1710–84) and Carl Philipp Emanuel (1714–88) were both to become noted musicians in their own right.

Bach travelled considerably while at Weimar – both on his master's business and his

Opposite *Portrait of Bach, painted in 1720 by Johann Jakob Ihle.*

own. When the court journeyed to Cassel in 1714, Bach played the organ at St Martin's church. A contemporary describes his virtuoso technique: 'His feet flew over the pedals as if winged, and loud notes roared like thunder through the church.' When the duke travelled to Weissenfels, Sebastian wrote a secular cantata for his birthday.

As an organist of great skill and growing reputation, Bach was frequently called away to inspect instruments, oversee refurbishments, and inaugurate new organs. We have an early description of his methods in inspecting an organ:

He was severe, but always fair, in his trials of organs. As he was perfectly acquainted with the construction of the instrument,

he could not be in any way deceived. The first thing he did in trying out an organ was to pull out all the stops and play with the full organ. He used to say in jest that he must know whether the instrument had good lungs. After the examination ... he generally entertained himself and those present by showing his skill as a performer. . . . He would choose a theme and express it in every one of the different forms of organ composition, never changing the theme, although he sometimes played for two hours or more without stopping. First he used the theme in a prelude and fugue, with the full organ. Then he showed his skill at using the stops for a trio, quartet, and so forth. Afterwards there followed a chorale . . . .

Bach's patron at Weimar, Duke Wilhelm Ernst of Saxe-Weimar.

Opposite The castle chapel at Weimar.

The Bastille Tower of the Wilhelmsburg palace, Weimar.

In 1717 Bach travelled to Dresden to compete with the French organist and composer Louis Marchand (1660–1722) in a keyboard contest, a popular contemporary form of entertainment. However, tradition has it that the Frenchman ran away, and Bach was accordingly judged champion by default. 'Obviously the Frenchman, so accustomed to being admired, must have found his ability unequal to the powerful assaults of his skilful and gallant opponent,' a contemporary German commented.

THE WEIMAR COMPOSITIONS

The result of nine years at Weimar spent largely at the organ is Bach's great body of works for that instrument, particularly the large-scale pieces known as fantasies, toccatas and preludes, usually climaxing in a fugue. We still have some 39 major organ works from this period, and these great pieces remain the staple of many church organists' repertoires, mainly because they represent the writing of a master organist.

A number of these pieces arise out of the organist's need to be able to improvise at his instrument during short gaps in church services – at entrances and exits of priests, patrons and other dignitaries, and other similar points. The compositions arising out of such needs are typically quite simple, often consisting of an arresting opening followed by a development in the form of variations in key, rhythm or other features. Similarly the intricate fugues of the Weimar years seem to arise from the young maestro's own skill and energy at the keyboard – and at the pedals, for Bach's organ writing demands virtuoso work from the feet as well as the hands.

Bach was also open to new influences. When copies of Vivaldi's concertos were brought to Weimar, with their innovatory foregrounding of the virtuoso violinist, and three clearly defined separate movements, Bach, possibly encouraged by the duke, arranged some of them for the keyboard. In so doing, Bach appropriated some of Vivaldi's musical structures for his own compositions – whether orchestral, organ or choral.

Antonio Vivaldi (c. 1675–1741), whose concertos influenced Bach's compositions during his Weimar years.

31

Bach's ambitions (and growing fame) are clearly evident. In 1713 he was invited to become organist at the Church of Our Lady at Halle, having played a test recital on the magnificent organ there, which boasted three manuals and 63 speaking stops. A contract was drawn up, but instead of taking the position, which he then found offered no increase in salary, Bach apparently used the evidence of his popularity to persuade Duke Ernst Wilhelm to promote him to Konzertmeister at Weimar and raise his salary. When the committee at Halle wrote to protest that Bach had simply used their offer to improve his situation at Weimar, he replied: '. . . my gracious master . . . already holds my service and my art in such regard that there is no need for me to travel to Halle to improve my salary here.' (By 1716 the authorities at Halle had evidently forgiven

him, and Bach accepted their invitation to inspect their newly completed organ.)

His new position at Weimar as Konzertmeister meant Bach had now also to direct the court orchestra and compose a monthly cantata for the chapel. The resulting cantatas contrast with those he had written while at St Blasius', Mühlhausen. There he was writing for a town church, with its own Pietistic leanings, and had at his disposal a well-trained choir but indifferent solo voices; here at Weimar he was writing primarily for his patron, the Duke of Weimar, whose tastes were broader and possibly more operatic, and for musical forces consisting of well-trained instrumentalists (a string quartet, skilled bassoonists and oboists, military trumpets and drums), a group of accomplished solo voices, but rather a poor choir. These factors help explain the

The original manuscript for a Bach Prelude & Fugue. Note the corrections at the foot of the first page.

style of the Weimar cantatas.

Some of the best of the surviving Weimar cantatas are set to the fine florid texts provided by Salomo Franck, court secretary and librarian at Weimar, and consist of several sections set as arias or recitatives. The cantatas are reminiscent of contemporary operatic music – though Bach must have had little opportunity to hear opera. However, he tended to use the full orchestra throughout, whereas operatic recitatives were normally accompanied simply by bare chords from the keyboard. Also, Bach's cantatas often end in a hymn, set simply or

elaborately: 'Jesu, joy of man's desiring' at the end of Cantata 147 is probably the best-known example in the English-speaking world. Yet Bach's cantatas cannot be truly called operatic. He wrote for the small, skilled group of chamber musicians at his disposal at Weimar, often countering a solo voice with a solo instrument.

It has become commonplace to see Bach as a deeply religious man, whose most profound works reflect a personal spirituality. However, it is important to recognise his role as a journeyman musician, responding to the requirements of his current employer.

A group of 18th-century chamber musicians.

Duke Ernst August of Saxe-Weimar, Wilhelm Ernst's more cultivated nephew.

At Weimar he wrote secular as well as religious cantatas: in fact the famous aria 'Sheep may safely graze' comes from his 'hunting cantata', *Was mir behagt*, a double dialogue between Diana and Endymion and Pan and Pales, written for the birthday of a friend of the duke. At Weimar, then, Bach broadened his canvas and showed himself to be a composer who could meet most exigencies.

When the aged Kapellmeister, Johann Samuel Drese, died in December 1716, Bach almost certainly felt he should receive the final promotion from Konzertmeister. However, the duke looked elsewhere, inviting the fashionable composer Georg Philipp Telemann, Kapellmeister of Frankfurt-am-Main, to take up the position. Although Telemann apparently turned down the offer, Bach still seems to have felt snubbed – Telemann was similar in age and experience to Bach – gave up writing new cantatas, and once more started to look for employment elsewhere. (In the event, Drese's untalented son Johann Ernst was appointed new Kapellmeister at Weimar.)

There was another reason for Bach's unsettledness. Duke Wilhelm's nephew, Duke Ernst August, lived in buildings adjoining his uncle's palace, and Bach was often attracted to spend time at his livelier, culturally more stimulating court. The jealous Duke Wilhelm started to fine members of his court who visited Ernst August's Red Castle, an act calculated to annoy an independent and obstinate man like Bach.

After successfully securing a new appointment elsewhere, Sebastian finally found himself languishing in a Weimar jail. In 1716 Duke Ernst August married the sister of Prince Leopold of Anhalt-Cöthen. With the help of members of the ducal family, Bach was appointed Kapellmeister to Prince Leopold, with an income of 400 thalers a year, as compared with the 250 thalers he was earning at Weimar. But Bach's request for release from his current employer was met with outright refusal, in part owing to the bad blood between the two dukes. When, in November 1717, Bach had

the temerity to ask Duke Wilhelm Ernst a second time for his release, he was thrown into jail:

On 6 November the sometime Konzertmeister and organist Bach was confined in the County Judge's prison for arguing too insistently for his release, and finally on 2 December released with dishonourable discharge.

CÖTHEN

B ach, at last a Kapellmeister, often recalled his contentment at the court of Cöthen, where, as he later wrote, he had 'a gracious prince who both loved and knew music, and in his service I intended to spend the remainder of my life.' This contentment was despite the fact that his new employer, Prince Leopold, was a Calvinist, and so required little music for the simple church services. The Victorians portrayed Bach as a devout Lutheran, never happier than in a church organ loft; however, recent writers tend to see Bach as primarily a professional musician with an eye always on the main chance.

Cöthen, some 60 miles north of Weimar, offered Bach a court orchestra of 18 players, including seven from the recently disbanded Berlin Court orchestra; the same salary as that of the Court Marshal; and a sympathetic patron in the person of the 24-

year-old prince, who had himself studied music in Rome, played the clavier and viola da gamba, and was a good bass singer. It was Prince Leopold who had built up the court orchestra from scratch, starting with three musicians employed to perform chamber music with him. Bach had greater freedom at Cöthen than at Weimar; there was no old Kapellmeister to whom he had to defer, nor were there the monthly cantatas to compose. Such cantatas as were required were often for secular events.

Bach's family was growing fast; they did not live in Leopold's moated residence but in a rented house nearby in the town of Cöthen. Sometimes orchestra rehearsals were held at the family home. Bach sent his sons to a new Lutheran school founded by the prince's mother.

THE CÖTHEN COMPOSITIONS

O ne of Bach's missions while at Cöthen was to visit Berlin to find a new harpsichord for the prince. While there, the Margrave Christian Ludwig of Brandenburg apparently requested some music from him; the result was the famous set of six compositions now known as the *Brandenburg Concertos*. Bach completed these in 1721 and dedicated them to the duke – though there is no record of any

A contemporary engraving of Cöthen.

Christian Ludwig, Margrave of Brandenburg, to whom Bach dedicated the six 'Brandenburg' concertos.

reward or remuneration accruing to the composer.

Much of the music composed at Cöthen is more direct and contemporary in style than his earlier elaborate church compositions; Bach seems to have picked up the influences of contemporary dances and of instrumental concertos such as those of Vivaldi. Many concertos of a similar nature date from Bach's time at Cöthen, including the set of *Brandenburg Concertos*, at least two violin concertos, and the double violin concerto. Bach contrasts with Vivaldi, however, in his peculiar way of orchestrating his concertos for different combinations of instruments.

Some of Bach's concertos feature no single instrumentalist, and for him the word 'concerto' meant simply a concerted piece.

The French style – like the French language – was becoming fashionable among the German aristocracy. Bach responded with a number of French suites after the style of the French composer Lully, and much 'French' dance music for the harpsichord or clavichord. Bach lacked a good organ at Cöthen (the palace organ had just 13 stops) and therefore devoted much of his keyboard playing and composition of this period to these stringed instruments, both known as the *clavier* in German. Some of his

Below *Giovanni Battista Lully, the French composer whose style Bach followed in some of the French suites written at Cöthen.*

Right *18th-century chamber musicians perform around the clavichord.*

Bach's original manuscript of a prelude from The Well-Tempered Clavier.

new works were intended for recital performances; others (like the *Little Keyboard Book for Wilhelm Friedemann*) were for use in teaching keyboard skills to the sons of the nobility and to his own family.

But Bach was not overly influenced by new fashions. He was still writing keyboard music in his old style, with two or three threads of melody with differing rhythms playing simultaneously. It was with testing pieces like this that Johann Sebastian passed on his keyboard techniques to his son Wilhelm Friedemann.

Another great work dating from Bach's Cöthen years is *Das wohltemperierte Clavier* (The Well-Tempered Clavier) – 'Preludes and Fugues through all the tones and semitones . . . for the use and profit of young musicians anxious to learn as well as for the amusement of those already skilled in this art. . .' – a set of 24 preludes and fugues for keyboard, one in every minor and major key, written for instruments tuned in the new way, by which every tone or semitone interval was roughly equal. (Under the old system, each key had its own subtle differences of tuning.) These pieces are not mere mathematical exercises but brilliant keyboard compositions – as the youthful Beethoven discovered when learning to play the fortepiano.

Also dating from the Cöthen years are a set of unusual unaccompanied sonatas for the violin and another set written for the cello. It is possible the violin suite was for the virtuoso violinist Pisendel of Dresden.

James's church, Hamburg, a city renowned for its fine organs and organists. However, the Hamburg committee appointed an unknown musician – after receiving a payment from him of 4,000 marks. Bach had been unwilling – and probably unable – to match this bribe, and continued in his position at Cöthen. But one of Bach's contemporaries,

Bach's great contemporary, George Frederick Handel (1685–1759).

It was while he was at Cöthen that Bach came nearest to meeting his great contemporary, George Frederick Handel – born in the same year as Bach and only 30 miles from Eisenach, at Halle. In 1719 Bach heard that Handel was visiting Halle while on a continental trip to find opera singers to perform in London; Leopold lent Bach a horse, and he set out to meet the composer. But Handel had already left on his return journey to England.

A NEW POSITION

As we have seen, Bach seemed relatively content at Cöthen, yet in 1722 we find him moving to Leipzig. What had happened to disturb his contentment? In July 1720, while he and his master were away on a visit to the spa of Carlsbad with a small band of musicians, Bach's wife Maria Barbara died suddenly. (It has been suggested she died in childbirth.) Bach arrived back to find his wife buried. It seems they had enjoyed a good marriage; the shock of his wife's death must have deeply stirred him.

Bach's immediate reaction was to apply for a job elsewhere. He made it clear he was interested in the post of organist at St

Johann Mattheson, later wrote contemptuously of the Hamburg congregation's treatment of Bach:

I remember . . . that a few years ago a certain great virtuoso, whose abilities have since brought him a handsome cantorship, presented himself as a candidate for the post of organist in a town of no small size, displayed his playing on the most various and greatest organs, and aroused universal admiration for his ability. But there presented himself at the same time . . . the son of a well-off artisan, who was better at preluding with his thalers than with his fingers, and he

Bach pictured with three of his sons.

obtained the post . . . despite the fact that almost everyone was furious about it. This all took place at Christmas, and the eloquent preacher, who had not agreed with the choice, expounded splendidly on the music the angels uttered at the birth of Christ. He managed to use this sermon to voice his thoughts about the recent rejection of the musician, and he closed by saying something like this: 'I am convinced that if an angel from Bethlehem came down from Heaven, and, wishing for the post of organist at St James's, gave a perfect recital, but had no money, he might as well fly off right away.'

While in Hamburg for the test performances, Bach once more met Reincken – now nearly 100 years old – and played for him on the organ at St Catherine's. The old master was impressed by Bach's improvisations on the old Lutheran chorale *An Wasserflüssen Babylon*: 'I thought this art was dead,' he is claimed to have said, 'but I see it still lives in you.'

On 3 December 1721 the 36-year-old Bach married Anna Magdalena Wilcke, the 20-year-old daughter of a court trumpeter at Weissenfels and herself a trained musician and member of the choir at the nearby court of Anhalt-Zerbst. Bach was a widower with four children; at the least they needed a mother, but in Anna Magdalena he seems also to have found a competent musician and a true companion. In the two *Little Keyboard Books* Bach compiled for his wife during the first four years of their marriage we find a little love poem, probably written by him, and certainly addressed to his wife:

> Your slave I am, sweet maiden bride,
> God give you joy this morning!
> The wedding flowers your tresses hide,
> The dress your form's adorning,
> O how with joy my heart is filled
> To see your beauty blooming,
> Till all my soul with music's thrilled,
> My heart's with joy o'erflowing.

However, Bach finally decided he had to

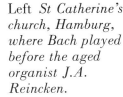

Bach's manuscript for a prelude from one of the 'Little Keyboard Books' written for his second wife, Anna Magdalena.

Left *St Catherine's church, Hamburg, where Bach played before the aged organist J.A. Reincken.*

leave Cöthen when, in 1721, the prince married his cousin Friederika Henrietta, daughter of Prince Carl-Freidrich of Anhalt-Bernburg. Bach soon discovered she was unmusical, and felt 'that the musical interests of the said Prince had become somewhat lukewarm. . . .'

In June 1722 Johann Kuhnau, the cantor at St Thomas's school at Leipzig, died. The post, which Kuhnau had held for 20 years, was very prestigious, and the town council short-listed six experienced musicians, finally choosing George Philipp Telemann to succeed him. However, Telemann's employers in Hamburg refused to release him, and raised his pay instead.

Bach had not originally applied for the post – Telemann was a personal friend – but now made his interest in the job known. The Leipzig authorities now chose as cantor Christoph Graupner, court musician of Darmstadt; but they were again frustrated by their candidate's employer, the Landgrave, who similarly refused to release him. Eventually the Leipzigers appointed Bach, who obtained a generous release from his own employer, Prince Leopold:

We have had in our service and under our patronage the respectable and learned Johann Sebastian Bach, since 5 August 1717, as conductor and director of our chamber music. We have at all times been very satisfied with his execution of his duties. . . .

LEIPZIG

Bach's final career move brought him to St Thomas's school at Leipzig, where he spent stormy years as cantor while creating a vast series of cantatas and much other church music.

On 5 May 1723 Bach signed a contract comprising 14 separate clauses outlining his duties as cantor at St Thomas's school, Leipzig; a fortnight later his family moved from Cöthen to Leipzig – needing two carriages and four wagons to convey them and their belongings. In moving to Leipzig, Bach was coming to the second city of Saxony, the centre of the German printing and publishing industries, and site of a progressive and famous university.

Distant view of the city of Leipzig.

Opposite The interior of St Thomas's church, Leipzig.

Right *St Thomas's school (left), close by St Thomas's church; a 19th-century engraving.*

Below *A 17th-century bird's eye view of the city of Leipzig. St Thomas's church is numbered '2' on the engraving.*

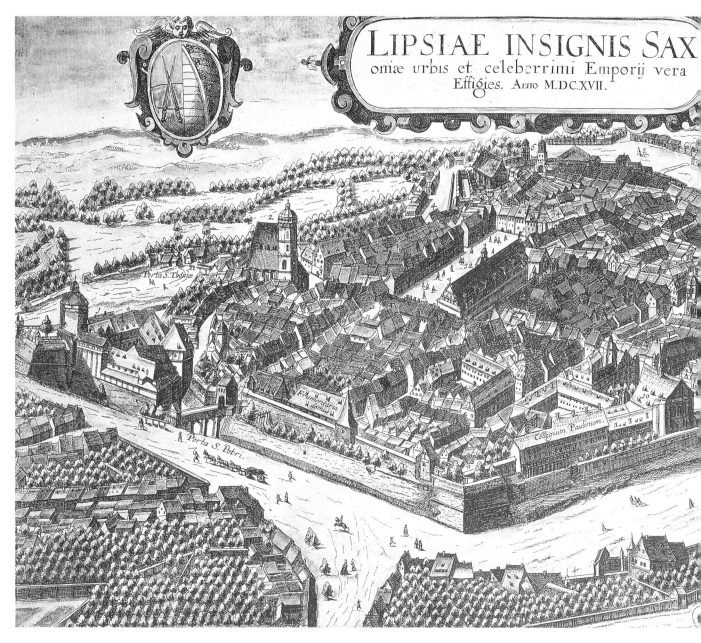

LIPSIAE INSIGNIS SAX
omiæ urbis et celeberrimi Emporij vera
Effigies. Anno M.DC.XVII.

Bach's appointment was as cantor of St Thomas's school, which was closely linked physically and organisationally to St Thomas's church. However, he had no official standing in that church; indeed, many of his works were performed in St Nicholas's, the other principal church in Leipzig.

The post of cantor of St Thomas's school was among the most important in Germany, making Bach responsible to the city council as director of music at the city's main churches, providing music for certain civic events, and supervising music in all the city churches, including St Thomas's, St Nicholas's, St Peter's, the New Church and for certain services at the university church of St Paul's. Bach had to direct the main choir at St Thomas's and St Nicholas's on alternate Sundays, oversee the organists and other musicians at both churches, and also

take responsibility for the music and instruments. For all this, his salary amounted to only a fraction of what he had received at Cöthen; but fees from weddings, funerals and so on increased it substantially, so that he was able to earn considerably more at Leipzig.

The cantor was third in rank at the school, behind the headmaster and deputy head, and among his duties as schoolmaster were to teach music and other subjects to boarders in the upper school, and to teach individual pupils performing skills. As a member of staff, the cantor also acted as duty master one week in every four, taking responsibility for discipline, waking the pupils at five each morning, leading morning prayers, supervising school meals, and generally running the place.

St Thomas's school had around 60 boarders, aged between 11 and the early 20s, who provided the choristers for the city churches. These boarders, mainly from deprived backgrounds, and maintained at the school on a charitable basis, had to sing outdoors at funerals, and in the city streets for alms, whatever the weather.

Not surprisingly, Bach was not enthusiastic about many of the non-musical tasks he was expected to fulfil as cantor, and soon persuaded one of his colleagues, Carl Friedrich Pezold, to take on most of his non-musical teaching duties, in exchange for a fee of 50 thalers per year. (The council had agreed to such an arrangement prior to appointing Bach, but later criticised him for it.) Bach also delegated to some of his school prefects: singing classes and sometimes even music for weddings were put under their direction.

When Bach came to Leipzig, he found the school in a sorry state. The headmaster, Johann Heinrich Ernesti, a well-regarded scholar in his time, was now 71 and had lost all control of staff and pupils. The school was inadequately housed, with insufficient beds for the 60-odd boarders (boys sometimes shared a bed), one classroom for three classes (and school dinners), and infectious diseases rife. Teaching standards had also plummeted.

The Bach family found themselves living in the same building as the boarders, the cantor's study separated from the sixth-form room only by a plaster divide. Anna Magdalena bore five children between 1723 and 1728, though only two survived early childhood. The growth of the family seems to have necessitated alterations in the cantor's residence in St Thomas's school in the winter of 1726.

1. Arx Pleissenburgum. 7. Frumentaria domus. 13. Cella Arcis.
2. Templum S. Thomæ. 8. Collegium nouum. 14. Sympoterion.
3. Quæstorum. 9. Collegium magnum. 15. Templum S. Nicolai.
4. Porta Francischanorum. 10. Templum Paulinum. 16. Taberna pannorum.
5. Templum Franciscanor. 11. Collegium S. Petri. 17 Schola S Nicolai.
6. Porta Randina. 12. Curia. 18. Schola S Thomæ.

THE CANTATAS

Notwithstanding these difficult domestic arrangements, Bach's first years in Leipzig seem to have been creatively rich, even inspired. There was no quarrel at Leipzig with Bach's musical ability; soon after he arrived it was recorded that '. . . the new Cantor and Director of the Collegium Musicum, Mr Johann Sebastian Bach, who has come here from the prince's court at Cöthen, produced his first music here, with great success.'

The sheer amount of music required for the main Sunday service at Leipzig was astonishing. Bach was responsible for the following musical items in the weekly Lutheran service, which started at seven in the morning, and, with an hour's sermon in the middle, probably did not finish until about 10.30: an organ voluntary or hymn, a Latin motet or organ voluntary, the *Missa*, an organ interlude, a hymn, a cantata, the hymn 'Wir glauben all' (the creed in metre), two hymns, and a Latin motet or hymn during communion. Though of course

St Thomas's church, Leipzig.

much of this music was already available, it all had to be arranged and practised under Bach's direction.

But there was no corpus of cantatas to be drawn from for the services: most of those performed at Leipzig during these years seem to have been written by Bach specially for the occasion. He would set the selected scripture text for the day for choir and orchestra, the musicians consisting of pupils from St Thomas's school, the town musicians and some university students. During these first years at Leipzig, Bach's greatest energy seems to have been devoted to composing; between 1723 and about 1729 he wrote a new cantata at a rate of nearly one per week, not to mention motets, the Passions, the *Magnificat* and much else, and all achieved while simultaneously rehearsing, directing and performing the music at the two principal churches, St Thomas's and St Nicholas's.

Bach wrote a new cantata for every Sunday, plus special cantatas for the major festivals in the church's year, totalling some 60 cantatas per year. He maintained this rate

Interior of St Thomas's, Leipzig.

Georg Philipp Telemann, who was chosen before Bach as cantor of St Thomas's school, though his employers refused to release him.

of output for his first five years at Leipzig, in that time completing about 300 cantatas, of which roughly 200 have survived. Yet after this initial burst of creativity, he wrote very few new cantatas.

Bach's cantatas were considerably more elaborate than those of his peers. Telemann often wrote cantatas simply for a solo singer; Bach's cantatas normally consisted of four-part choruses; arias, frequently with taxing parts for solo instruments such as the oboe (apparently accomplished oboists were available in Leipzig); and recitatives with complex orchestral accompaniments. In 1727 Bach met a Leipzig teacher and poet named Christian Friedrich Henrici, who, under the pen name Picander, provided the libretti for a number of the Leipzig cantatas. Henrici complimented the 'incomparable Kapellmeister' on the beauty of his music.

But Bach's output at Leipzig was not restricted to cantatas. During his first Christmas in Leipzig, 1723, Bach's first known setting of the *Magnificat* was performed, using a structure rather similar to the cantatas, with a chorus to open, followed by arias, and finishing with a choral setting.

The following Christmas, Bach wrote the *Sanctus in D major*, now familiar as a movement in the *B Minor Mass*. This setting blazes brilliantly, utilising a six-part choir, oboes, and dramatic high trumpets.

THE PASSIONS

Bach's major new work of 1724 was the *St John Passion*, written for performances at Easter that year. Bach arranged for his *St John Passion* to be heard at St Thomas's church; however, the superintendent of St Nicholas's church complained about this to the city council, since it had previously been etablished that the Easter Passions would be performed in alternate years at the two churches, and in 1724 it was the turn of St Nicholas's. When Bach explained that there was not enough room for the musicians in the choirloft at St Nicholas's, and that the harpsichord was broken, the council agreed to remedy these matters, while Bach promised not to make such arrangements in future without first consulting the superintendent.

The tradition of Passion Music during Easter Week dates back to medieval Germany, when different singers represented the main characters in performances of the Easter story. In Protestant Leipzig, the texts for the Passion music were taken largely from Scripture, with the addition of arias and congregational hymns. Bach's predecessor at Leipzig, Thomas Kuhnau, had in 1721 set a precedent for Bach by writing Passion Music for Good Friday.

Bach's *St John Passion* is marked by its concise, dramatic nature, the chorus representing the fickle Jerusalem crowd, now sorrowful, now mocking Christ; and the narrative driven on by the solo Evangelist. Bach scored his *Passion* for an orchestra of two flutes, two oboes, a bassoon, strings and continuo, viola da gamba, lute, and two viole d'amore.

The culmination of this period – and possibly of Bach's entire career – is the ambitious *St Matthew Passion*, probably written for Good Friday 1727. For this massive work, Bach's collaborator Picander (who was also Leipzig's postal commissioner) wrote the non-scriptural additions to the text, while Bach composed for large forces comprising two choirs of 20 voices, plus two orchestras of at least 12 musicians. Reflecting the length of St Matthew's passion narrative, the work is much longer than the *St John Passion*, and comes across as rather more contemplative in style than the dramatic earlier Passion.

In 1725 Bach started a second *Little Keyboard Book* for Anna Magdelena, filling it with arrangements, arias and other occasional pieces. It was at this time, too, that Bach began to publish some of his keyboard work. In 1726 came the first of his series of partitas, suites for accomplished players.

Meanwhile, Bach had not dropped his contacts with Cöthen, and even continued to write occasional pieces for the prince, making guest appearances there with his wife. Then in March 1729 Bach took his wife and eldest son, Wilhelm Friedemann, to Cöthen

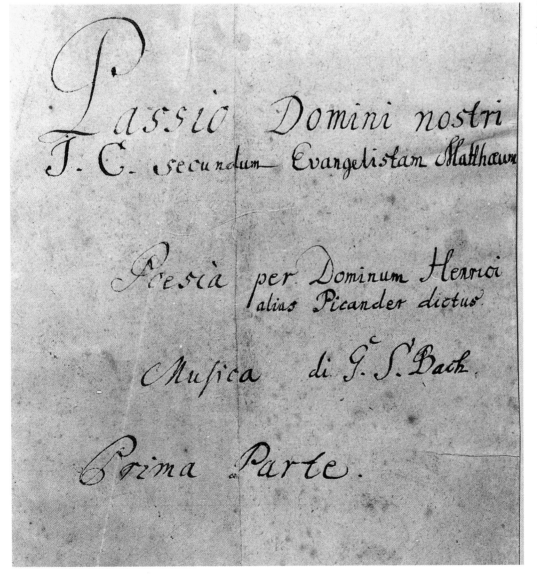

The title page of Bach's St Matthew Passion.

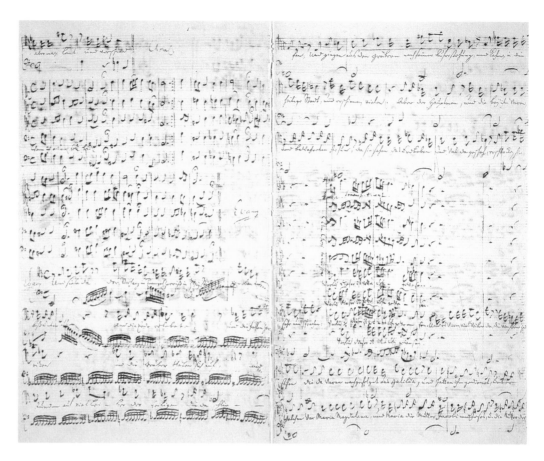

Bach's original manuscript for his St Matthew Passion.

to perform his cantata *Klagt, Kinder, klagt es aller Welt* at the funeral of his former employer, Prince Leopold. They received a generous fee of 230 thalers for this final assignment.

Bach had continued to refer to himself by the courtesy title of Kapellmeister von Haus of Cöthen after coming to Leipzig. With the death of Leopold, he looked for another court to attach himself to. In February 1729 Bach spent several days at the court of Duke Christian of Weissenfels, and was in due course granted the title Kapellmeister to the court of Saxe-Weissenfels.

These years find Bach at possibly his most active. In addition to his formidable output of new music, and his musical direction in Leipzig, he was still much in demand as an organ recitalist and inspector of instruments, and we discover he visited Störthal, Gera and even Dresden to inspect or inaugurate new organs.

THE
LEIPZIG DISPUTES

While these first years at Leipzig were marked by a prodigious creative output, they were also marred by a series of clashes with authority. We have already noticed that Bach frequently ran

into controversies with his earlier employers; this pattern was always likely to repeat itself in Leipzig, where he was answerable to several different authorities – to the headmaster of St Thomas's school, to the city council, to the church consistory. Such restrictions must have constantly irked the composer, particularly after the relative freedom he had enjoyed at Cöthen.

The musical arrangements at the university church of St Paul's were the subject of Bach's first clash with the Leipzig authorities. In 1710 the university had introduced a new weekly Sunday service at St Paul's, to be supervised by that church's own musical director. However, Bach's predecessor, Kuhnau, had insisted that he should continue to direct the old service at the church, and receive the fee of 12 gulden. After Kuhnau's death Johann Gottlieb Görner was appointed director of both old and new services at St Paul's. Soon after his appointment as cantor in 1723, Bach appealed to the university council for the traditional rights to direct the old service to be restored.

Bach was always single-minded in the pursuit of his rights. Although his first petition to the council was rejected out of hand, further negotiations resulted in his being offered the old service, but at only half Kuhnau's fee. Bach was still not satisfied: he appealed to Augustus, Elector of Saxony, in Dresden and in 1726 he was finally granted

The organ of St Thomas's church, Leipzig.

Below *Frederick Augustus, Elector of Saxony.*

Opposite *Bach's petition to Leipzig city council, 1730.*

the old service at the old fee. Bach then seems to have lost all interest in St Paul's church and its services, apart from occasional special events there. The university authorities for their part retaliated by depriving Bach of valuable musical commissions.

One of the special events at St Paul's precipitated another noisy dispute, again involving Görner, the musical director at the university church. In 1727 an aristocratic student named Hans Carl von Kirchbach proposed a memorial service at the university church to mark the death of the elector's wife, Christiane Eberhardine. He commissioned the libretto for a funeral ode from Johann Christoph Gottsched, a poet and university teacher, and asked Bach to set this to music. Once the music was ready, Görner and the Leipzig university authorities tried to prevent Bach from taking part in the ceremony for which the music had been composed. Eventually Kirchbach paid off Görner with 12 thalers, and Bach directed his own composition at the keyboard, steadfastly refusing to sign the statement demanded by Görner that he would never again make private arrangements with members of the university.

But disputes continued to mark Bach's

career. In 1728 he argued with the sub-deacon at St Nicholas's about who should choose the hymns at vespers. When Bach appealed to the church consistory, they backed their minister, telling the cantor he should abide by the sub-deacon's choice of hymns.

Finally, in 1730 matters came to a head when Bach was presented with a list of complaints about his cantorship, including absence without permission, neglect of the daily singing classes at St Thomas's school, and various other criticisms and infringements. In his response, once more we find evidence of Bach's intransigence. Rather than trying to explain himself, or attempting to arrive at a compromise, he simply submitted a memorandum to the council, outlining the shortcomings *he* found in the musical resources allocated to him in Leipzig:

A short but indispensable sketch of what constitutes well-appointed church music, with a few impartial reflections on its present state of decline.

For well-appointed church music, singers and instrumentalists are necessary. In this town the singers are provided by the foundation pupils at St Thomas's school,

The university church of St Paul's, Leipzig, where J.G. Görner was musical director.

Kurtzer, iedoch höchstnöthiger Entwurff
einer wohlbestallten Kirchen Music; nebst
einigen unvorgreiflichen Bedencken, von
dem Verfall derselben.

Zu einer wohlbestallten Kirchen Music gehören
Vocalisten und Instrumentisten.
Die Vocalisten werden hiesiges Ohrts von denen
Thomas Schülern formiret, und zwar von vier
Sorten, als Discantisten, Altisten, Tenoristen
und Bassisten.
So nun die Chöre derer Kirchen Stücke recht, wie
es sich gebühret, bestallt werden sollen, müßen
die Vocalisten wiederum in zwey Sorten
eingetheilet werden, als: Concertisten und
Ripienisten.
Derer Concertisten sind ordinaire 4, auch
wohl 5, 6, 7 biß 8; so man nehml. per Choros
musiciren will.
Derer Ripienisten müßen wenigstens auch
achte seyn, nehmlich zu ieder Stimme zwey.
Die Instrumentisten werden auch in unterschie-
dene arten eingetheilet, als: Violisten,
Hautboisten, Fleutenisten, Trompetter
und Paucker. NB. Zu denen Violisten
gehören auch die, so die Violen, Violoncelli und Violon
spielen.

and are in four sections: trebles, altos, tenors and basses. If the choirs are to perform church music properly . . . the singers must be subdivided into two groups. . . .

There are 55 boarders at St Thomas's; they are divided into four choirs for the four churches where they perform vocal and instrumental music, and sing motets and chorales. All the pupils who sing at St Thomas's, St Nicholas's and the New Church need musical training; for St Peter's, it is only necessary to be able to sing chorales.

Each choir needs at least three trebles, three altos, three tenors and three basses, so that if one is unable to sing (which often happens, particularly at this time of year, as is evident from the prescriptions the doctor sends to the dispensary) there are

at least two voices for each part to sing the motet.

The instrumental forces required are as follows: two or three first violins; two or three second violins; two first violas, second violas and cellos; a double bass; two or three oboes; one or two bassoons; three trumpets; and one drum: a total of at least 18 instrumentalists. However, church music often requires flutes too, so we need two flautists: the grand total amounting to 20 musicians.

The city employs eight musicians for church music: four pipers, three violinists, and an apprentice. Discretion forbids me from speaking plainly about their competence and musical knowledge; however, I should say that they are semi-retired, and far from as well-rehearsed as they should be. Their forces then consist

A coloured engraving of the church, school and consistory of St Thomas's, Leipzig.

of: . . . two trumpets, two violins, two oboes and one bassoon. So that means that we lack the following players: two first violins, two second violins, two violas, two cellos, two flutes and one double bass. Until now university students and pupils from St Thomas's school have made up the difference; they used to

Above *Two 18th-century woodwind instruments: an ivory treble recorder (top) and a wooden treble recorder.*

be very willing to do this, hoping they might in due course receive a gratuity. But since the small payments they once received have now been stopped, their willingness has also ceased; for who is going to give his services gratis?

In addition, I can't omit mentioning that a large number of boys who are musically unskilled and ignorant have been admitted to the school, with a consequent decline in the quality of performances. A boy who knows nothing about music, and can't even sing a second part . . . will never be any use musically. And even the boys who have some basic knowledge don't become useful as quickly as I want. . . . No time is allowed for training them . . . as soon as they enter the school, they are put in a choir. . . .

The result is easy to see . . . I have no chance of getting the music into better shape.

Joh. Seb. Bach

(The letter ends with a list of boys, with an adjoining candid note of their musical ability.)

This extraordinary document has been quoted at some length, since it not only throws light on Bach's quarrel with the city authorities, but also affords fascinating details about the arrangements for music in an 18th-century German city. Bach's comments about the quality of the boy singers are borne out by his experience earlier the same year, when auditioning applicants for nine vacant places at St Thomas's school. Bach listened to 23 candidates, rejecting 11 as totally useless. The council then proceeded to appoint four of these no-hopers, together with five whom Bach had not heard at all, and only five of the boys whom Bach had selected. The cantor can hardly be blamed in the circumstances for feeling slighted!

It may seem absurd now that a major composer such as Bach should have been provided with such poor musical resources, but we should not lose sight of Bach's own recalcitrance and 'incorrigible' behaviour, nor of the fact that many of the city councillors had wanted a teacher rather than a musician as cantor at St Thomas's. The immediate upshot of this dispute was that the council decided to deprive Bach of some of the perks of his position. The other inevitable result was that their cantor once more started to look elsewhere for a better situation.

Two months later we find Bach writing to his old school friend of Ohrdruf days, Georg

Erdmann, now living at Gdansk and acting as legal adviser to the Russian court. To this friend, living so far away, Bach could afford to be frank about his situation:

. . . So God ordered it that I should be called here as director of music and cantor at St Thomas's school. Now at first it didn't seem to be right to become cantor after having been Kapellmeister, and I put off my decision for three months. But this post was described to me so favourably that in the end (and particularly because my sons seemed likely to become students) I took the risk, in God's name, and came to Leipzig, took the test and accepted the *mutation*. And here I have remained till now, following God's will. But since now (1) I find this position is not as remunerative as it was described to me; (2) many of the additional fees accruing to the post have been withdrawn; (3) the cost of living is very high here; and (4) the authorities are odd, and show little interest in music, with the result that I have to live with almost continuous irritation, envy and harassment, I shall be compelled, with the help of the Almighty, to seek my fortune elsewhere. . . .

The letter culminates in Bach's requesting Erdmann to put in a word for him in Gdansk, in the hope that a suitable, and well-paid, job could be found there. (Incidentally, Bach also complains to his old school-friend of the fluctuation of fees from funerals at Leipzig, which become rarer when 'the air is healthy'!) Whatever lay behind this request to his friend – and we do not know if Bach had a specific post in Gdansk in mind, or whether or not Erdmann replied – Bach was never in fact to leave Leipzig.

We cannot finish with this letter to Erdmann without quoting from Bach's final paragraph, where he offers a charming and intimate portrait of his family:

My eldest son is a law student, the other two are still at school, one in the first and the other in the second class, and my eldest daughter is still unmarried. The children of my second marriage are still young; the eldest is a boy, aged six. But they are all natural musicians, and I assure you that I can make up a vocal and instrumental ensemble from my family, especially as my wife sings a very pleasing soprano, and my eldest daughter can also join in well enough. . . .

Opposite Interior *of St Thomas's church, Leipzig.*

THE
FINAL YEARS

Bach's last years saw more controversies, more disputes, increasingly private compositions, but little recognition by his contemporaries.

The year 1730 seems to mark a water-shed in Bach's career. After this date the flood of new church music created in his early years at Leipzig dwindles to a trickle. Bach's interest in liturgical music seems to wane drastically; but we need to remind ourselves that he was not wedded exclusively to the organ loft. In total, less than a quarter of his creative life was devoted to church music.

Detail of the decoration on a clavichord belonging to Bach.

Opposite Portrait of Bach by Elias Haussmann, 1746.

THE COLLEGIUM MUSICUM

In the spring of 1729 Bach found a new sphere for his musical energies when he took over the Collegium Musicum society in Leipzig, which had been founded by the composer Telemann in 1702, when he was organist at the New Church. This society, which numbered among its members Leipzig students, professional musicians, and probably older members of Bach's own family, met on Friday evenings at Zimmermann's coffeehouse in the Catherinenstrasse – and in his suburban garden in summer. This Collegium Musicum often provided the music for university or royal events, sometimes the occasion for special pieces by Bach.

Doubtless the weekly meetings of the Collegium Musicum featured performances of Bach's earlier chamber music, orchestral suites and other music, some of it composed while he had been at Cöthen. But Bach's new output consisted of a number of concertos, mainly surviving as arrangements for keyboard and strings, but originally written for violin and oboe soloists. These harpsichord concertos – sometimes for two or three keyboards – mark the origins of the genre of keyboard concertos, which soon burgeoned into the popular piano concerto of the classical and romantic eras of the next hundred years. But despite the quality of these works by Bach, they failed to reach a wider contemporary public than that at Leipzig. His famous *B Minor Suite* for flute and strings, written in the French style, came later in the 1730s.

But there was also vocal music, and it was probably at Zimmermann's coffee-house that Bach's humorous cantatas, *The Contest between Phoebus and Pan* and the *Coffee Cantata*, were first performed. The former work, with a libretto by Picander, Bach's regular collaborator, is a satirical attack on musical criticism and musical fashions; in it

Part of Bach's manuscript for his Coffee Cantata.

Midas listens to a singing competition between Phoebus and Pan, and is given donkey's ears for judging a superficial contemporary-style aria sung by Pan to be true art. We are probably not mistaken in finding a reflection of Bach's own attitude to modern styles in Midas's reward.

The *Coffee Cantata*, first performed in 1734 or 1735, concerns a coffee addict (the subject doubtless tickled Zimmermann's fancy) who agrees to give up the beverage if her father permits her marriage – though she also extracts a promise that she and her future husband will be allowed to pursue their caffeine indulgence. These cantatas are the lightest, most amusing works of Bach's to survive.

Later, in 1742, among other secular cantatas, Bach wrote a 'cantata burlesque', popularly known as the *Peasant Cantata*, to honour a new lord of the manor on an estate outside Leipzig. In this work, which (uniquely for Bach) utilises folk idioms, the composer shows he was conversant with and adept at contemporary musical fashions.

There were a few religious works in this period, but Bach more often revised or rearranged earlier cantatas. At Christmas 1734 the six cantatas comprising the *Christmas Oratorio* were performed for the first time on various days between 25 December and 6 January (Epiphany). This music is characterised by its tenderness rather than any drama or passion.

A NEW HEADMASTER

The elderly head of St Thomas's school, the ineffective Ernesti, died in the autumn of 1729, to be replaced by Johann Matthias Gesner, a younger and enlightened man whom Bach had known at Weimar. He admired Bach's gifts and shared his views on the place of music in the life of the school, declaring that 'our ancestors intended the school to be a seminary of music whereby the singing in all our

Johann Matthias Gesner (1691–1761), the enlightened head of St Thomas's school.

Portrait (1760) of Wilhelm Friedemann Bach (1710–84).

churches might be provided.' Gesner encouraged the boys to practise their music, arguing that praising God in music linked them to the heavenly choirs. (Those unconvinced by logic were persuaded by fines.) He also restored to Bach the perks that the council had deprived him of, and officially relieved him of all teaching apart from music. Gesner was clearly fond of Bach, and he left a sketch of the cantor directing music from the keyboard:

... singing with one voice, and playing his own parts, but watching over everything and bringing back to the rhythm and the beat, out of 30 or even 40 musicians, one with a nod, another by tapping his foot, a third with a warning finger; giving the right note to one from the top of his voice, to another from the bottom, and to a third from the middle of it – all alone, in the midst of the greatest din made by all the participants, and, although he is executing the most difficult parts himself, noticing at once whenever and wherever a mistake occurs; holding everyone together, taking precautions everywhere, and repairing any unsteadiness; full of rhythm in every part of his body – this one man taking in all these harmonies with his keen ear and emitting with his voice alone the tone of all the voices. . . .

Gesner soon made his presence felt, and started by enlarging the school premises, Two storeys were added to the school building, relieving the pressure on space; the rebuilt school was re-opened in 1732. The Bachs had to move temporarily to a house in Hainstrasse while the rebuilding work was carried out.

Seven more Bach children were born between 1730 and 1742, though three of them died in infancy. Of the others, Johann Christoph Friedrich later worked at the court of Bückeburg, and Johann Christian became known as the 'London' Bach. Bach's eldest son, Wilhelm Friedemann, finished his university studies in 1733 and was appointed to the post of organist at St Sophia's, Dresden, at the age of 23. This was at a time when his father was cultivating the Dresden connection; Sebastian had himself

given organ recitals at St Sophia's, and also directed performances of the Collegium Musicum there.

COURT COMPOSER

When the Elector Friedrich August I died in 1733, Johann Sebastian wrote a Kyrie and Gloria, later to be incorporated into the *B Minor Mass*, and presented them to the new elector, Friedrich August II. There was a strategy to Bach's activity: the Dresden court was Roman Catholic, so the Mass was particularly welcome; and with the music, he presented a petition, outlining his problems at Leipzig:

Left *Friedrich August I, Elector of Saxony.*

Above *Johann Christian Bach (1735–82) in his middle years.*

I have had for some years and until now the directorship of music in the two main churches in Leipzig, but have had to endure various undeserved affronts, and at the same time reduction in the fees connected with the position, which injuries could cease completely if Your Royal Highness were to grant me the favour of bestowing on me the title of Your Highness's Court Kapelle. . . .

However, Bach's plan misfired, and no new title was forthcoming, although he continued to write works in honour of the royal family, including Abendmusik (vespers) to mark the anniversary of the elector's accession to the throne of Poland, performed when the elector visited Leipzig in 1734. The royal guests were serenaded by the orchestra in a concert lit by torches held by 600 university students.

In September 1736 Bach once more appealed for a title to the court at Dresden, and this time his petition was granted: he was declared Court Composer, and soon began signing his letters accordingly.

MORE DISPUTES

However, in 1734, only four years after taking up the post, Gesner resigned the headship of St Thomas's school and left to become a professor at the University of Göttingen. Gesner's successor was Johann August Ernesti (1707–81) – no

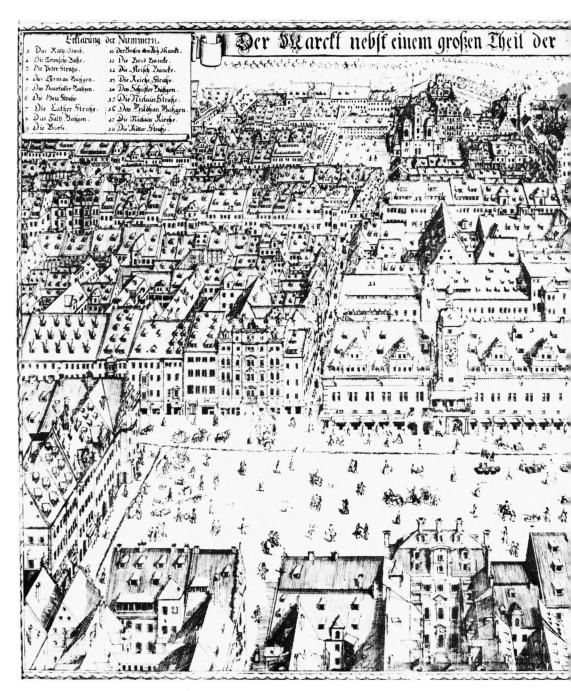

relation to Gesner's predecessor. Aged only 27, Ernesti represented the new wave of enlightened thought, and planned to transform St Thomas's school into a progressive academy. Music did not figure in his scheme; it was alleged that he would discourage boys he found practising the violin saying: 'Surely you don't want to become an alehouse fiddler, too?'

Although Bach at first got along well with the young head, asking Ernesti to become godfather of Johann Christian in 1735, their contrary views on music were destined to precipitate conflict. The trouble began in 1736. The head prefect had beaten a boy so harshly that Ernesti expelled him. The headmaster then immediately appointed a new prefect without consulting his cantor,

Bach, for whom it was vital that the prefects were musical so that they could help keep the musical programme running at the four city churches.

As usual, the dispute burgeoned, with charges and counter-charges, even coming to fisticuffs in the choirloft when Bach forcibly removed the prefect whom Ernesti had appointed (he was incompetent musically). Only in April 1637 did the city council pronounce on the matter, laying blame about equally on the headmaster and the cantor. But Bach was not satisfied, and continued to argue his case, even appealing directly to the Elector Friedrich August.

While Ernesti was certainly too dictatorial, Bach underlined his customary dogged combativeness. Once more we see him

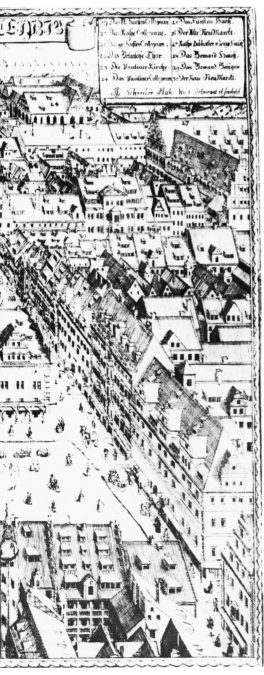

Left *Bird's-eye view of the market square, Leipzig.*

Above *Johann August Ernesti (1707–81), head of St Thomas's school.*

tenaciously defending what he saw to be his rights, employing all means, including decidedly antique byelaws, to defend his case, and neglecting his statutory duties – the head prefect conflict had first arisen because Bach had failed to fulfil a wedding engagement in person.

Hardly had the Ernesti affair blown over than Bach's son Johann Gottfried was causing his father concern. In 1735

Sebastian had helped his son into the post of organist at St Mary's church, Mühlhausen, but Johann Gottfried quickly ran into debt, causing his father to pay his debts and to use his influence to help him get another organist's position, at St James's church, Sängerhausen. But Bach's son had not learned his lesson, ran into worse debt, and fled into hiding. The unfortunate Johann Gottfried survived only briefly, dying of

A sentimental domestic scene in the Bach household, as conceived by the late 19th-century painter T.E. Rosenthal.

fever in 1739, after entering the University of Jena.

We are afforded a little more light on the Bach household during these years, since in 1737 Bach's nephew, the 33-year-old Johann Elias, came to live with them, working as Sebastian's secretary and as tutor to the younger children. Elias's letters throw sideways glances on the family; he was evidently fond of Anna Magdalena, several times ordering carnations as a gift for her, trying to buy a linnet to sing for her, and also asking his own family to send sweet wine to Leipzig as a thank-you to his host's family.

Despite this apparent domestic contentment, the public controversies continued. In May 1737 the composer and musical theoretician Johann Adolf Scheibe launched an anonymous attack on Bach's music in his Hamburg magazine *Der Critischer Musikus*, accusing Bach of losing touch with contemporary fashions in music. While recognising Bach's skill as a performer, as well as his technical prowess as a musician, Scheibe singled out his over-use of ornamentation and excessive counterpoint as symptoms of his allegedly turgid and laborious music:

This great man would be the wonder of the universe if his compositions displayed more agreeable qualities, were less turgid and sophisticated, more simple and natural. His music is extremely difficult to play because the skill of his own limbs sets the standard for him; he expects singers and players to be as agile with voice and instrument as he is with his fingers, which is impossible.

Bach did not reply to this attack himself, but was defended by a lecturer at Leipzig University, J.A. Birnbaum, and later by Christoph Lorenz Mizler, founder of the Society of Musical Sciences. The dispute has sometimes been seen as a personal attack by Scheibe, motivated by revenge for being deprived of an organist's post where Bach was among his examining committee. But only a couple of years later Scheibe was lavishing praise on Bach's *Italian Concerto*, 'a piece which deserves emulation by all our great composers'.

In the main substance of his criticism, Scheibe was in fact expressing the opinion of his time – that Bach's embellishments, counterpoint, and intricate musical textures were beginning to sound somewhat outdated and provincial. A new musical age was dawning.

THE LATE WORKS

After this, Bach wrote little for public performance. How far this was due to a recognition that he was no longer writing to contemporary tastes is unclear. The works he produced were private pieces, not intended for public performance, as is true too of Beethoven's last years. When

Potsdam in the 18th century, where Frederick the Great held court.

there was a dispute about the Passion music for Easter 1739, Bach declared that performing a Passion was 'only a burden' to him. The works of his last years were for himself – not for the church, the city, the Collegium Musicum or anyone else.

Bach did continue his duties as cantor, delegating where possible. He continued to accept pupils for individual tuition, and adopted one, Johann Christoph Altnikol, as a particular protegé: Altnikol later married Bach's daughter, Elisabeth Juliana Friederika. Bach also continued to inspect organs: he examined the instruments at St John's church, Leipzig, in 1743, and at St Thomas's in 1747, as well as others outside the city. His reports were not always favourable; after examining the organ of St Wenceslas's church, Naumburg, he stated:

It will be necessary for the organ builder to be asked to go over the whole organ again, from stop to stop, aiming for greater equality of voicing and of key and stop action . . .

THE VISIT TO BERLIN

In 1747 Bach undertook one of his most prestigious visits. His son, Carl Philipp Emanuel, had been appointed harpsichordist to Frederick the Great of Prussia in 1740, and in 1747 Emanuel's wife was expecting their second child. Apparently the king had been pressuring Emanuel to bring his father to the court at Potsdam: evidently by now the old man's fame was spreading. With two good reasons to make the journey, with Wilhelm Friedemann, Johann Sebastian set out for Frederick's court outside Berlin.

Wilhelm Friedemann later recounted the visit to Bach's biographer, Forkel:

At this time the king used to have every evening a private concert, when he himself usually performed some concertos on the flute. One evening, just as he was getting his flute ready, and his musicians

Right *Frederick the Great of Prussia (1712–86).*

Right *Frederick the Great plays the flute at a chamber concert at Sans-Souci, Potsdam.*

Below *Bach plays the organ for Frederick the Great.*

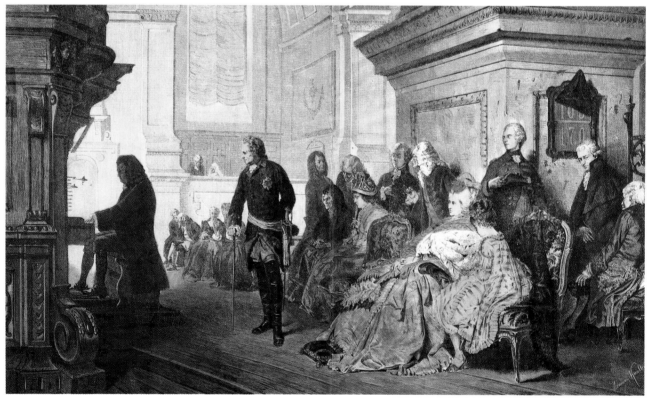

The rococo palace of Sans-Souci, Potsdam.

were assembled, an officer brought him the written list of the strangers who had arrived. With his flute in his hand, he ran over the list, but immediately turned to the assembled musicians and said, with a kind of agitation: 'Gentlemen, old Bach is come.' The flute was now laid aside; and old Bach, who had arrived at his son's lodgings, was immediately summoned to the palace. . . .

The king gave up his concert for this evening, and invited Bach, then already called the Old Bach, to try his fortepianos, made by Silbermann, which stood in several rooms of the palace. The musicians went with him from room to room, and Bach was invited everywhere to try and play extempore compositions. After this had gone on for some time, he asked the king to give him a subject for a fugue, in order to execute it immediately without preparation. . . .

The next day Bach was taken to all the organs in Potsdam, as he had before been to Silbermann's fortepianos. After his return to Leipzig, he composed the subject, which he had received from the king, in three and six parts, added several artificial passages in strict canon to it, and had it engraved, under the title *The Musical Offering*, and dedicated it to the inventor.

Bach himself had 100 copies of this work printed, giving many away to friends, and selling the rest for one thaler each. The *Musical Offering* consists of a three-part fugue, a six-part fugue, two sets of five canons, and a sonata in four movements. A presentation copy, on special paper, was sent to Potsdam, though we have no record that the king rewarded Bach in the normal manner.

In this same year Bach finally joined the Society of Musical Sciences, founded by the polymath Lorenz Christoph Mizler, sometime one of Bach's music students. This corresponding society also numbered among its distinguished members the composers Telemann, Handel and Graun, and

Bach probably wrote some of his late works with the intention of circulating them among its members. Some of his late, mathematically complex, works must have impressed this group of musical intellectuals.

THE LAST WORKS

Much of Bach's time in his declining years was devoted to reordering and organising into final form some of his earlier works. He worked on a companion volume to *The Well-Tempered Clavier*, although the first volume remained unpublished; this second set of 24 preludes and fugues was completed in 1742, as part of Bach's signing-off process.

He was also publishing keyboard music; a series of *Keyboard Exercises (Clavier-Übung)* had been appearing during the 1720s, culminating in the 30 *Goldberg Variations*, named after a pupil of Bach, for whom they are supposed to have been composed, and commissioned by the Baron von Kaiserling, Russian Ambassador to the court at Dresden. They are notable for their beauty as much as for the virtuoso playing they require, and reflect a mind almost obsessed with mathematical regularity and

This title page of the first edition of Bach's Keyboard Exercises (Clavier-Übung), 1726.

precision, every third piece being a canon (or 'round') of great ingenuity. (Bach was clearly pleased with the results; when Elias Gottlob Haussmann painted his portrait in 1746, Bach chose to hold one of the six-part canons in his hand.)

The *B Minor Mass* was completed around 1749, bringing together sections dating from various earlier periods. These included the *Sanctus* first performed on Christmas Day 1724, at St Thomas's church, and an *Agnus Dei* originally written as an aria for an Ascension Day oratorio in 1735, and a new setting of the Nicene Creed. This enterprise affords another example of Bach's commitment to 'tidying things up'.

From about 1745 Bach was preparing the *Art of Fugue* for publication, though it was still unfinished when he died, and seems to have been written for instruction and a puzzler's satisfaction rather than performance – the music is not adapted for any particular instrument.

DEATH

As early as June 1749 the First Minister at Dresden had ordered that a new candidate for cantor should be selected 'in case . . . Bach should die'. We do

*Clavier Übung
bestehend in
Praeludien, Allemanden, Couranten, Sarabanden, Giquen,
Menuetten, und andern Galanterien;
Denen Liebhabern zur Gemüths Ergoezung verfertiget
von
Johann Sebastian Bach,
Hochfürstl. Anhalt-Cöthnischen würcklichen Capellmeister und
Directore Chori Musici Lipsiensis.
Partita I.
In Verlegung des Autoris
1726.*

not know if this means that the old man was already in ill health, although there is little evidence of illness during his life. However, by the next year Bach's eyesight was failing rapidly, and in March his cataracts were treated by a celebrated English oculist, John Taylor (who also operated on Handel). A second operation had to be undertaken several days later, but the net result of this treatment was complete loss of sight.

Bach lived on until July the same year, when he was suddenly 'seized by a stroke . . . followed by a burning fever'. He died, aged 65, on 28 July 1750, and was buried three days later in the graveyard of St John's church, Leipzig.

Even in death the Leipzigers failed to recognise the stature of their cantor. 'Bach was certainly a good musician, but no school teacher,' they grumbled; and they resolved never to repeat their error in appointing an accomplished musician: 'The school needs a

Bach at 60 (1745).

Opposite *Bach memorial at St Thomas's church, Leipzig.*

cantor – not a conductor.' The new appointee was Gottlob Harrer, the recommendation of the court of Dresden, and a man who seemed to promise a less turbulent term of office.

Since Bach had died intestate, his property had to be divided between his wife and surviving children in proportions set down in law. Anna Magdalena asked permission to live on for six months at the school, and for a guardian to be appointed for the five children still living at home. The inventory drawn up of his property shows that Bach possessed, *inter alia*, five harpsichords, two lute-harpsichords, 10 string instruments, a lute and a spinet.

Bach's musical manuscripts were divided roughly in half between his eldest sons; those going to the careful Carl Philipp Emanuel have largely survived the years; those going to the dissolute Wilhelm Friedemann have partly been lost. Anna Magdalena lived on for 10 years more, unsupported by her stepsons, and dying a poor almswoman in 1760.

In what is an unusually warm memoir by a son, Carl Philipp Emanuel helped Johann Friedrich Agricola publish a portrait of his father in 1754. They concluded that Sebastian had a fine musical ear; that as a conductor he 'was very accurate, and uncommonly sure of the tempo, which he usually took at a lively pace'. They extolled his virtuosity at the keyboard: 'With both feet he could play things with the pedals which many skilled *clavier* players would find it hard enough playing with five fingers.'

Emanuel wrote later of his father's accuracy in tuning: 'No one could tune his instruments to his satisfaction; he did it all himself. . . . He heard the slightest wrong note even in very large ensembles. . . . In his youth, and until he was nearing old age, he played the violin cleanly and penetratingly, and controlled the orchestra better with his violin than he could have done from the harpsichord.'

Although we have much of Bach's music, of his private life we really know little enough. We have only one authenticated portrait, that painted by Haussmann in 1746; and we have only one personal letter, together with the notes of Elias, his nephew. But a man who fathered 20 children, who enjoyed smoking his pipe, and who rarely turned visitors away, cannot be as stern as many have pictured him – though we have seen plenty of instances of his single-mindedness, which could easily turn to pig-headed obstinacy when obstructed. It is important not to over-emphasise his stubbornness or litigiousness. It is inevitable that we see more of the public man, fighting for his rights, than of the private, family man: we are almost entirely reliant on public and legal records for our evidence about Bach, since we possess only a handful of his personal documents.

As a composer Bach was pretty comprehensive in the different types of music he wrote, and original in his creativity. However, he was not a man to forge new structures or styles; indeed in his last years he might almost be said to have become stylistically reactionary.

Although Bach made many career moves during his working life, we may perhaps usefully divide his compositions into three periods: the period up to about 1713, when he was in effect completing his musical apprenticeship, building on his German predecessors; 1713–40, his period of mastery; and the late period, when his music becomes at once more cerebral and more inward-looking. But throughout his career Bach could produce works which are fearsome in their technical demands, requiring great virtuosity in the performer.

Of course the Bach name did not die out. The last Bach we know to have made a living from music was Wilhelm Friedrich Ernst, who died in 1845. But Johann Sebastian's three sons, Wilhelm Friedemann, Carl Philipp Emanuel and Johann Christian were all successful in their day. Johann Christian converted to Catholicism in his 20s, went to London, and was extremely popular for a time.

Carl Philipp Emanuel Bach (1714–88), who wrote an affectionate memoir of his father.

BACH'S MUSIC

With a vast body of work ranging from miniatures for solo instrument to choral works, modern interpretations of Bach range from authentic to unshamedly modern.

Like most composers of his time, at his death Johann Sebastian Bach was quickly forgotten: he was already being overtaken by musical fashions during his last years. But as early as 1780 a revival of interest in his work began. At first this movement was restricted to musical and intellectual circles in Vienna; but Haydn, Mozart and Beethoven all knew something of, and learned something from, Bach's music. He was finally beginning to be recognised as a composer rather than primarily as a performer or teacher.

Early in the 19th century one of the pioneering non-professional choirs, the Berlin Singakadamie, began to perform some of Bach's motets. In 1829 the young Mendelssohn conducted the first posthumous performance of the *St Matthew Passion* – though with various changes to make it more acceptable to the romantic ear. Mendelssohn's own work, and especially his choral compositions, were influenced by Bach; while Brahms, Lizst and Bruckner all learned from, and acknowledged directly or indirectly, Bach's influence. In the 20th century, composers as varied as Bartók, Webern, Schoenberg, Stravinsky and Hindemith have been influenced by Bach.

During most of the two centuries since his death, Bach has been regarded as a devout Lutheran, whose music is overwhelmingly pietistic and spiritual in nature; and until quite recently, he was seen as a quintessentially German composer. Albert Schweitzer, a great scholar and organist as well as the celebrated 'Doctor of Lamabaréné', even saw his music as a coded mysticism, 'a phenomenon of the reality of the inconceivable'.

Albert Schweitzer (1875–1965), a celebrated Bach performer and theoretician.

Opposite *Statue of Bach at his birthplace, Eisenach.*

BACH'S MUSIC

By 1900 a collected edition of his complete extant works, begun in 1850 by the Bach Society in Germany, was finished. However, with the start of a new, and more scientifically researched, complete edition of Bach's works in 1954, there came a new recognition of Bach as first and foremost a professional musician, meeting deadlines, responding to the various requirements of church, city council or court, and adapting or improvising as need be.

Along with this rediscovery there has come the new search for authenticity in

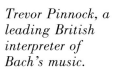

Trevor Pinnock, a leading British interpreter of Bach's music.

performance: the instruments, the scoring, the ornamentation, the number of voices, the techniques are all carefully researched, so that, as nearly as possible, the performance sounds much as Bach would originally have envisaged it. Such performances rediscover a freshness and clarity lost in the sounds of the huge orchestras and choirs to which 20th-century audiences have become accustomed.

The Brandenburg Concertos

We have seen earlier that these six famous concertos are named after the Margrave of Brandenburg, to whom they were dedicated by Bach. However, they had not originally been conceived as a group by the composer, and in fact differ widely in their musical structure, expression, and even in the in-

struments for which they were scored. Yet all six *Brandenburgs* follow Vivaldi's concerto pattern, and may be compared with that composer's sets of six concertos.

The first *Brandenburg Concerto* was written for strings, continuo, two horns, three oboes, bassoon and violin – a very unusual instrumental combination. Such a skilled harnessing of the varied and contrasting tone colours of different instruments was a particular gift of Bach's, and dazzles by comparison with Vivaldi's less adventurous, and perhaps less sympathetic, scoring. Bach created this first concerto largely by skilfully cannibalising some of his own earlier music. Its French style – like the French dedication notice to the Margrave – was probably calculated to appeal to that aristocrat's sophisticated tastes.

The second concerto brings together at first glance another odd group of solo

The English Concert in performance.

The Academy of St Martin-in-the-Fields in performance.

instruments – violin, oboe, recorder and trumpet. Bach has sometimes been criticised for writing for such unorthodox combinations, and in particular for the lack of balance between the shrill trumpet and the gentle recorder – but on original instruments, and in a small 'chamber', the sound would not be so unbalanced as such critics claim.

The third *Brandenburg Concerto* contrasts strongly with its predecessors, in that it is scored only for strings – which divide into nine separate parts – together with bass continuo. However, the fourth and fifth concertos are markedly more conventional, and were probably written a little later than the rest. In the fourth, the solo instruments consist of two recorders and a violin, which latter instrument tends to predominate in performance; in the fifth concerto, the solo

instruments consist of violin and flute, but in fact the harpsichord emerges from its usual role as continuo and takes the long cadenza.

The sixth and final *Brandenburg Concerto* is scored for two violas, two bass viols, cello, violone and harpsichord continuo; it has been suggested that this economical scoring made it especially suitable for the little band of musicians Prince Leopold of Cöthen used to take with him on his visits to the spa at Carlsbad.

Overall, the eccentric and varied instrumentation of the different concertos meant that the musical resources required by the Margrave of Brandenburg to perform all six adequately had to be quite extensive; he must have been a little surprised to receive such a gift. Yet the joyful exuberance of the *Brandenburg Concertos* seem to reflect the

The Bach Orchestra in performance in the Old Town Hall, Leipzig.

happy, contented life that Bach led at Cöthen. until the death of his first wife, and his patron's marriage to a woman who had little inclination to music.

The Violin Concertos and the Concerto for Two Violins (the 'Double')

Bach wrote the majority of his concertos during his years at Cöthen. Presumably the solo parts in the A minor and E major violin concertos were written for the leader of the Cöthen court orchestra, Joseph Spiess, who would have been joined in the double violin concerto (in D minor) by Martin Friedrich Marcus. Both men had been recruited by Prince Leopold from the disbanded Berlin orchestra.

The beautiful *Concerto in D minor for*

Two Violins features a superb duet linking the two outer movements, and characterised by overlapping, imitative phrases. All three violin concertos are structured in three movements, like those of Vivaldi, though Bach as ever brings a freshness and invention to the form.

The Well-Tempered Clavier (The 48)

The first book of the *Well-tempered Clavier (Das wohltemperierte Clavier)* dates from 1722, as we have seen earlier, and consists of a series of 24 preludes and fugues, one in each minor and major key. The name of the collection denotes the fact that it was possible to play them all without re-tuning the keyboard. Their completeness owes something to an evident need Bach displays for mathematical symmetry; but they also add to a tradition of composing such keyboard works in all 24 keys. Today they are often performed as a complete cycle, though it is doubtful that such performances were undertaken in Bach's own time.

Bach wrote a second set of 24 preludes and fugues in 1742, though the name *Well-Tempered Clavier Book 2* has been added by others. He perhaps used this second grouping to bring together various pieces he had written since the first collection, for it seems to form part of the 'tidying up' process of his later years. The *48*, as the two books are often called, require great concentration from the performer: as a young keyboard player, Beethoven found them to be very engrossing.

Anna Magdalena Bach's Little Keyboard Books (Clavierbüchlein)

By contrast with many of the works discussed, these are miniature, and charmingly domestic, collections of keyboard music; their title has been often wrongly translated into English as 'Notebooks'. Bach's affection for his young second wife, Anna Magdalena, is reflected in the two little books, in which he collected a selection of keyboard music for her.

In the first book, some of the pieces were compositions of his own, others arrangements he had made of other composers' music. They include little minuets, gavottes and other dance forms, together with chorale settings and arias (doubtless to be sung by his gifted wife).

The second book for Anna Magdalena Bach contains the makings of the five so-

Martha Argerich, a distinguished modern interpreter of Bach.

called French suites, which are among the easier keyboard music Bach wrote. Though simple, they retain musical interest, and have survived, since both music teachers and music pupils find them useful and attractive. Also contained in this second *Keyboard Book* is the aria which was later to be used as the theme of the *Goldberg Variations*, the beautiful aria 'Bist du bei mir', and some compositions by Bach's older sons.

Suite No 2 in B Minor

This suite, perhaps the best-known of the four orchestral suites by Bach, is written in the French style, and features an attractive and glittering solo part for the flute. (The flute was very fashionable at the French court of Versailles.) The four suites were not regarded as a group by Bach, but all have a strong French flavour, and consist of a French overture, followed by a series of light dance-like movements such as gavottes, minuets, bourrees and so forth. The second suite culminates in a very fast *badinerie*, a favourite showpiece for flautists. The third suite, in D major and for full orchestra, includes another piece which has become famous by itself; the so-called 'Air on the G string', so-called after it was arranged for performance on the G string of the violin.

The Passions

A tradition of singing the Passion story during Holy Week dates back to medieval times, and continued in Germany after the Reformation, when the Lutheran churches began to stage more dramatic Passions than the simple plainchant of the Middle Ages. It seems that Bach wrote five Passions in all, though only the *St John* and the *St Matthew* have survived. He certainly wrote a *St Mark Passion*, performed in Leipzig in 1731; the other missing Passions may be a *St Luke* (though the evidence is ambiguous), and a single-choir version of the *St Matthew*.

The *St John Passion* was first heard at Easter 1724 at St Nicholas's church, Leipzig, and was performed again the following year at St Thomas's. The *St Matthew Passion* may have been performed for the first time in 1727, and we know it was performed again in 1736 and in the 1740s, with some small changes.

Both Passions are structurally similar. Soloists representing the Evangelist, Jesus, and other characters such as Peter and Pilate, together with a chorus representing the crowd, tell the story of the arrest, trial, crucifixion and burial of Christ, mainly using settings of the chosen Gospel narrative. These parts of the Passions are simple and dramatic; they are intended to push along the narrative vividly.

The Monteverdi Choir in performance with the English Baroque Soloists under the direction of John Elliot Gardiner.

Below The Leipzig Gewandhaus Orchestra with the Thomaner Choir perform Bach at Leipzig.

Alongside this, the Passions include a number of lyrical arias, which are decidedly more contemplative and introspective in nature, dwelling on the meaning of the Passion story for the individual Christian believer. In this way, the Passions maintain a creative tension between the historical events in Jerusalem and the believer's contemporary response.

But the Passion music was not written to be listened to in a concert hall; we must remember that it was part of the liturgy, for performance on that most solemn of days in the Christian calendar, Good Friday. For this reason there were also places within the music for congregational participation. For this purpose, a number of chorales, well-known Lutheran hymns with new settings by Bach, were included; the hymn now widely known as the 'Passion Chorale' appears five times during the course of the *St Matthew Passion*.

In addition to the recitative narrative, the arias, and these chorales, both Passions open and close with monumental choruses, respectively to set the tone and provide an appropriate ending. The opening chorus of the *St Matthew Passion* is particularly impressive in scale.

As we saw earlier, it is often claimed that the *St John Passion* is more dramatic than the *St Matthew*; however, there are places in the *St Matthew* too where drama is vivid in the extreme. The greater length of the *St Matthew Passion* is of course in part due to the greater extent of the passion narrative in

St Matthew's Gospel. For many music lovers, and not solely for Christian believers, the *St Matthew Passion* is Bach's most impressive and profound work.

The Goldberg Variations

Originally known simply as an *Aria with Variations*, this set became known by its present title after Bach's early biographer Forkel recounted the story that the variations were commissioned to be played by Johann Gottlieb Goldberg, the young harpsichordist to Count Keyserlingk of Dresden, to ease his patron's insomnia. The story seems far-fetched, for these are pieces for a virtuoso, and would be more likely to shock someone into alertness by their brilliance than to lull them to sleep!

The theme of the *Goldberg Variations* is taken from the second *Anna Magdalena Little Keyboard Book*, and may not be by Bach himself; but the 30 variations show Bach at his most brilliantly inventive, foreshadowing Beethoven in his mastery of this musical form. Every third piece in the set of variations is in the form of a canon; many of the variations are like songs or dances in style.

The B Minor Mass

Bach completed four short masses, though their dating, and the reason for their composition by a Lutheran composer, are both rich debating grounds for scholars. The *B Minor Mass* is contrasted with these four by its sheer grandeur, by its text (the short masses seem to have consisted only of a Kyrie and Gloria), and by the fact that it seems not to have been written for a particular performance so much as to draw together music worthy of the text. In fact some writers have suggested that Bach was aiming to bring together model movements for each section of the Mass – rather than create a massive single multi-movement work for performance.

Bach had sent the Kyrie and Gloria sections of this great work to the Elector of Saxony in Dresden in 1733, when he was angling for the title of Court Composer. For these sections, consisting of 11 movements, he had re-used parts of earlier cantatas and other choral works, but on a much more ambitious scale, and in an Italianate style which would be acceptable to the Catholic court of Dresden. Now he scored them for a five-part choir, and an orchestra which included drums and trumpets. When he came to write the Credo for his great Mass, Bach once more cannibalised earlier cantatas; while, as we saw earlier, the Sanctus re-used a setting for six choral parts originally written for Christmas 1724.

There are altogether 24 movements comprising this massive work, though probably only about six were specially written for it. The rest Bach adapted, altered, rewrote or plundered from earlier works, but still managed to create in the *Mass* a work of the highest achievement. The *B Minor Mass* is additionally remarkable in that it appears not to have been composed for specific liturgical use, being much too long, apart from anything else. It draws on both recognisably 'religious' music and on what is undisguisably dance music or lively concerto music.

THE SEARCH FOR AUTHENTICITY

The outcome of intensive recent research into Bach, and into 18th-century music in general, has been much new light on the practice of music-making in his time, and an attempt to approach more closely the performance effects of the period. Research has covered such technicalities as how to interpret the rhythms marked in the music, how to play the 'ornaments' marked in the original scores, how to accompany a solo instrument, and so forth. At the same time there has been extensive research into the nature and construction of baroque musical instruments, and into the specific techniques of playing them. Instruments of the period have been lovingly restored and exact replicas carefully constructed.

One of the pioneers of authenticity was Thurston Dart, who researched the original manuscripts and 18th-century music manuals in an attempt to rediscover the styles and techniques of the baroque instrumentalists. Dart, himself a fine keyboard player, was careful not to become merely pedantic in his research, but to create a performing edition that could sensibly be utilised by contemporary players. He edited a number of Bach's works, for instance preparing an edition of the *Brandenburg Concertos* in the version Bach wrote before ever he thought to send them off to the Margrave of Brandenburg.

In turn ensembles such as the Collegium Aureum helped pioneer this return to authentic musical textures using 'original instruments' and interpretative techniques, the resulting performances often revealing a new clarity and pace in the works, especially as a result of the care devoted to rhythmic vitality. Other ensembles which have ex-

Opposite *The English organist Peter Hurford has recorded the entire canon of Bach's works for the organ.*

celled in this revival of authentic performing styles include the English Concert, the Academy of Ancient Music and the Vienna Concentus Musicus. Less successful authentic performances can sound rather academic and lacking in warmth, with little variation in dynamic or expressiveness.

Some music-lovers find the sound of baroque stringed instruments unrelenting – even harsh – though the best performances and recordings escape this criticism. Similarly, baroque trumpets can sometimes sound strained in their upper register. Authentic performances of baroque music normally substitute the quieter one-keyed baroque flute or the recorder for the modern flute with its multiplicity of keys.

Trevor Pinnock, the conductor of the English Concert, and a fine keyboard player, at his best combines a high scholarship in rediscovering the authentic text for the works with excellent musicianship in performance, winning performances of high quality from the ensembles he directs. Another successful and stylish ensemble performing in the authentic mode is the Linde Consort, directed by Hans-Martin Linde, who on occasion plays the flute solo part himself. It is certainly not the case that an authentic performance has to lack expressiveness or true musical feeling: the great Dutch harpsichordist (and musical scholar) Gustav Leonhardt and the baroque violinist Sigiswald Kujiken have performed Bach's sonatas for violin and harpsichord with clarity and remarkable sympathy.

The Academy of St Martin in the Fields, established by Sir Neville Marriner, works with instrumental forces and musical styles close to those of the 18th century, but does not use 'authentic' instruments or instrumental techniques. Like other directors, Marriner often uses an edition of the music which he has himself researched; works such

as *The Musical Offering* demand decisions on the order in which the various pieces comprising it are performed. Like the Academy of St Martin, the English Chamber Orchestra, under Raymond Leppard, another fine smaller ensemble, uses modern instruments, but brings the findings of modern scholarship to their performing styles.

MODERN INTERPRETATIONS

Not all modern performances are on authentic instruments. Some contemporary pianists are beginning to reclaim Bach's harpsichord works: for example Andras Schiff, the young Hungarian pianist, heard in his childhood a record of the American pianist Glenn Gould play-

Otto Klemperer, who employed all the resources of the modern symphony orchestra in his thrilling interpretations of Bach.

Trevor Pinnock directs the English Chamber Orchestra from the keyboard.

Left *The German violinist Anne-Sophie Mutter, one of the best of the younger interpreters of Bach.*

ing Bach, and from that moment was convinced that Bach could legitimately be played on the piano.

Glenn Gould was himself committed to playing the Bach harpsichord works on the piano, and is famous for his idiosyncratic interpretations. He succeeds in playing the interweaving parts of Bach's fugues with great clarity and intense intelligence; but, for many listeners, his recordings are ruined by the distracting groans and croons of the artist. Schiff, Martha Argerich and the Russian pianist Andrei Gavrilov are all fine contemporary exponents of Bach on the piano, Schiff being careful to interpret Bach in baroque style.

Many other contemporary soloists interpret Bach's music on modern instruments; for example John Williams has recorded some of Bach's unaccompanied music for

Yo Yo Ma, who performs Bach's viola da gamba suites on the cello.

lute on the guitar, while Yo Yo Ma plays Bach's viola da gamba sonatas on the cello. Similarly the German violinist Anne-Sophie Mutter does not play a baroque violin, and brings a romantic warmth to the Bach violin concertos that some purists find misplaced. Nevertheless she is one of the finest contemporary performers of the Bach violin oeuvre.

Among organists, perhaps pre-eminent in recent years has been the English musician Peter Hurford, who has recorded the entire canon of Bach's works for the organ. Unlike the traditional German organists, who tend to play rather soberly, and sometimes with little tension, aiming for a clarity which will allow the complex strands of the fugues to be heard, Peter Hurford has great freshness, bringing out the colour and emotion of the

music in an almost orchestral approach. He manages to combine grandeur with meticulous attention to detail, giving performances of great vigour and imagination. His recordings have been made on various organs in different countries, each chosen for the particular sound it can lend the performance. Lionel Rogg has also recorded much of Bach's organ music, with a characteristic clarity and literalness rather than flamboyance.

A similarly comprehensive recording enterprise to Hurford's involves the Bach cantatas. In the early 1970s the first in a projected complete series of recordings of the Bach cantatas performed to the utmost authenticity was produced, and the series has been steadily built up in the intervening years. Authentic original instruments or precise replicas are used; boys' voices are employed instead of women's, for both choral and solo work; and the choirs and instrumental ensembles are confined to the size that Bach would originally have had at his disposal. As is the tendency with rigorous authenticity, in some instances the performances can verge on the pedantic and strained, but this venture, recorded by the Vienna Concentus Musicus, with Gustav Leonhardt and Nikolaus Harnoncourt, is at the very least an essential reference point.

Otto Klemperer's magnificent recording of the *St Matthew Passion* with the Philharmonia Choir and Orchestra contrasts utterly with such performances. Far from 'authentic' in the sense we have been discussing, since he employs the forces of a conventional 20th-century symphony orchestra, the whole performance is nevertheless pervaded by an intense devotion, created by the conductor, and picked up by the distinguished soloists, who include Peter Pears, Dietrich Fischer-Dieskau and Elisabeth Schwarzkopf.

THE MAVERICKS

Notorious among arrangers of Bach was Leopold Stokowski, who transcribed many of Bach's works for the modern symphony orchestra, recording the transcriptions with some of the large American symphony orchestras. The result is a flamboyant, inflated sound, highly enjoyable, but poison to the purist.

Among the most daring – and successful – performers of Bach in recent years have been Walter Carlos and Benjamin Folkman, who have arranged a number of Bach's works for the Moog synthesiser. The synthesiser captures well the spirited rhythms of Bach. Among the most exciting – and familiar – of these pieces are the arrangements of the *Brandenburg Concertos* – much used by radio stations as signature tunes! Like Stokowski's orchestral arrangements, this is not music for the purist; however, one recording, which included a selection of pieces, sold hugely in the United States, successfully introducing a new generation to Bach.

Leopold Stokowski, whose orchestral arrangements of Bach are calculated to shock the purist.

INDEX

94

PICTURE ACKNOWLEDGMENTS

Archiv für Kunst und Geschichte 6, 8–9, 12, 15 top, 15 bottom, 24–25, 26, 27, 34, 36–37, 39, 47, 48–49, 53, 54, 55 top, 62, 65, 66, 67 right, 70–71, 72, 74, 77, 78; Clive Barda 82, 82–83, 83, 86, 87 top, 88, 90–91, 91 bottom, 92, 93; Bavaria Bildagentur/Bavaria 11; Berolina 50, 80, 84–85, 87 bottom; Bildarchiv Preussischer Kulturbesitz 9 top, 42–43, 45, 58–59, 63 top, 74–75; British Library 32–33; Bomann Museum 16; Deutsche Staatsbibliothek 7 bottom, 25, 52, 76; EMI 91 top; E t Archive 63 bottom; Mary Evans Picture Library 31, 38, 48, 69, 81 bottom; Hulton-Deutsch Collection 40, 41; Kunstsammlungen zu Weimar 28, 29, 35; Kupferstichkabinett Dresden 37; Josef Makovec 13; Mansell Collection 17, 73, 75; Mansell-Alinari 9 bottom; Museum für Hamburgische Geschichte 14, 44–45; Music Library of Yale University 81 top; National Portrait Gallery 42; Nationale Forschungs- und Gedenkstätten Johann Sebastian Bach der DDR 56, 57, 61, 68–69; Royal College of Music 59; Sächsische Landesbibliothek/ Deutsche Fotothek 55 bottom, 67 left; Ullstein 10 top; VEB Deutscher Verlag für Musik Leipzig/Werner Reinhold 18–19, 19, 22, 23, 30, 46, 51, 79; ZEFA/H Lütticke 20, Strachil 7 top, 10 bottom.

JAMES PRENDERGAST LIBRARY

3 1880 0314336 8

780.92 D
Dowley, Tim.
   Bach

	DATE DUE	

JAMES PRENDERGAST
LIBRARY ASSOCIATION

JAMESTOWN, NEW YORK

Member Of

Chautauqua-Cattaraugus Library System